The Mass Comm Murders

The Mass Comm Murders

Five Media Theorists Self-Destruct

ARTHUR ASA BERGER

Illustrated by the Author

ROWMAN & LITTLEFIELD PUBLISHERS, INC.
Lanham • Boulder • New York • Oxford

ROWMAN & LITTLEFIELD PUBLISHERS, INC.

Published in the United States of America
by Rowman & Littlefield Publishers, Inc.
4720 Boston Way, Lanham, Maryland 20706
www.rowmanlittlefield.com

12 Hid's Copse Road, Cumnor Hill, Oxford OX2 9JJ, England

British Library Cataloguing in Publication Information Available

Library of Congress Cataloging-in-Publication Data

Berger, Arthur Asa, 1933–
    The mass comm murders : five media theorists self-destruct /
Arthur Asa Berger.
        p.   cm.
    Includes bibliographical references and index.
    ISBN 0-7425-1720-9 (cloth : alk. paper) —
    ISBN 0-7425-1721-1 (pbk. : alk. paper)
    1. Mass media.   I. Title.
    P90 .B4133   2002
    302.23—dc21   2001058729

Printed in the United States of America

♾ ™ The paper used in this publication meets the minimum requirements of
American National Standard for Information Sciences—Permanence of Paper for
Printed Library Materials, ANSI/NISO Z39.48-1992.

This book is dedicated to those scholars whose work, and in some cases whose friendship, convinced me that popular culture and the mass media were worth investigating: Roland Barthes, Umberto Eco, George Gerbner, Marshall McLuhan, and Aaron Wildavsky.

Contents

Acknowledgments

I would like to thank my editor, Brenda Hadenfeldt, for supporting me and offering some valuable suggestions for this book. I also am grateful to my copyeditor, Laura Larson; my production editor, Renee Jardine; and other staff members at Rowman & Littlefield for their invaluable assistance. Finally, I obtained some useful ideas and insights from some reviews of this book, before it was published, by three professors whose names are not known to me.

Author's Note

A few years ago Mitch Allen, president of AltaMira Press, asked me to write and draw a comic book on postmodernism. He thought a comic book would be a good way to get students interested in postmodernism. I found, however, that I could not work with the comic strip format, so, instead, I wrote a comic academic murder mystery, *Postmortem for a Postmodernist*. In a rather bold, audacious, and, to my mind, brave move (others, less charitable, might say foolhardy), he published the book. I'm pleased to say it has enjoyed a modest success and now is in its second printing.

I had so much fun writing the book that I started writing some others, including *The Hamlet Case* (www.Xlibris.com), which uses a cultural studies approach to analyze Shakespeare's greatest play, *Hamlet*. I wrote several other mysteries (all available at Internet booksellers) and then this book, *The Mass Comm Murders*, about mass communication theory. I would describe my mysteries as, both literally and figuratively, novel ways to reach and teach students. I've included an extensive bibliography at the end of this mystery so readers interested in reading more about mass communication theory will find many books to consult.

Now that I have redefined myself as a postmodernist novelist, I have taken liberties and, in the best postmodern tradition, made the book something of a collage or pastiche and inserted, here and there, brief passages from the works of famous mass communication theorists and other social scientists. Since this book is a mystery, I won't tell you who I took the quotes from or where they are. In addition to being a book on mass communication theory, I see it as a black comedy that's a parody of the mystery genre and a satire of academia—it pokes fun at the scholarly life. I manage to kill five professors in this book. I've discovered what many murderers have discovered: the more people (in my case professors) you kill, the easier it gets.

Some would argue that while I haven't actually killed anyone, I have, in some of my books and lectures, bored a number of people to death—or come close to it. I won't dignify that notion with a response.

This book is a work of fiction. All the characters and situations in this book were invented by me and are the products of my imagination. Any resemblance in this book to actual persons, dead or alive, is accidental and strictly coincidental.

The Mass Comm
Murders Personae

Elijah Ashdod-Sfard. An Israeli media theorist from the University of Tel Aviv who, though world famous, feels he isn't getting the recognition he deserves. He's also a bit of a snob. His claim to fame involves his work on the theory of the silent majority and the so-called silence spiral. "Yes," he thinks, "I've had considerable acclaim, but how come, of my great modesty, nobody says anything?" He is married to an Israeli sociologist, Shoshana Manishevitz, who also teaches at the University of Tel Aviv.

Nigel Haddley-Lassiter. A British scholar who has been to the best schools and after graduating with a first from Oxford felt that everything would be going downhill after that. He is a sociologist whose maxim "A sender sends a message to a receiver with X effects" has brought him great acclaim. He is forty years old and teaches at the London School of Economics while he waits for a call from Oxford or Harvard. His wife, Deborah Ginsberg, is a psychiatrist and playwright.

Mikhaila Blotnik-Kiev Vološinova. She is a beautiful Russian linguist, in her midthirties, from Moscow University. Her theory of dialogism has got her invited to lecture at universities all over the world. She has left a trail of broken-hearted media scholars who like her theories but like her and her vivacious personality even better. She also has left a trail of broken-hearted husbands, having been married and divorced four times.

Lisa Schauber Gurke. Lisa is an elderly German professor, rumored to be a bisexual and a spy, whose theory of mass media events received a great deal of attention by media theorists. She has interesting things to say about the television series *Survivor* and many other things. She teaches at the University of East Berlin and lives part of the year in Tokyo with a Japanese avant-garde novelist, Mimosa Rakutani.

Jean-Georg Simmul. He is a professor at Paris X whose theory of signs and hyperreality and work on postmodernism have made him a star in the American academic media and communications firmament. "America is a gigantic simulation, the most postmodern country in the world," he has argued, and he has written countless books to prove his point. He's a big favorite as a visiting professor at Yale and the University of California at Berkeley.

Solomon Hunter. He is an inspector in the San Francisco Police Department who has been involved in a number of cases in which academics have murdered other academics. He dresses in Brooks Brothers suits and is quite stylish. Hunter doesn't give anything away, which causes problems for the academics with whom he interacts—they don't know what to make of him.

Talcott Weems. He is a sergeant in the San Francisco Police Department and Solomon Hunter's right-hand man. Weems is narrow-minded, opinionated, and anti-intellectual. He has no hesitation in speaking his mind and doesn't think much of university types, especially postmodernists.

The Mass Comm
Murders

Stereotype/Stereotyping * The social classification of particular groups and people as often highly simplified and generalized signs, which implicitly or explicitly represent a set of values, judgements and assumptions concerning their behaviour, characteristics or history. * Initially introduced from the language of printing into that of the social sciences by Lippmann (originally published 1922, 1965), the concept has been developed particularly in social psychology, occupying a central place in the study of **cognitive** processes, **attitudes,** and **prejudice**. . . . Stereotyping in much of this work has been defined as a particular extension of the fundamental cognitive process of categorization, whereby we impose structure and make sense of events, objects and **experience.** This process in itself requires the simplification and organization of diverse and complex ranges of phenomena into general, **labelled** categories. . . . Stereotypes . . . not only identify general categories of people: **national** populations (i.e. the Irish), **races** (i.e. the Latin race), **classes** (i.e. the working class), **genders** (i.e. men or women), occupations (e.g. accountants) and **deviant** groups (e.g. drug-takers), etc. they are distinctive in the way they carry *undifferentiated* judgements about their referents.

—Tim O'Sullivan, John Hartley, Danny Saunders
Martin Montgomery, and John Fiske, *Key Concepts in
Communication and Cultural Studies,* pp. 299, 300

"It's a very sad story," thought Elijah Ashdod–Sfard.

"It's a very sad story," thought Elijah Ashdod-Sfard. He looked around the crowded room where he was moderating the panel on "New Developments in Media Theory." The panel members were all on an elevated stage, seated behind a table. There were stairs on either side of the stage, leading down to the room. There was a door near the front of the room, where the panel was taking place, and another door in the back of the room.

"It's sad. For the most part, the room is filled with a bunch of academic nobodies, leading lives of quiet desperation," he thought. "I hardly recognize anyone in the room. Maybe I'm getting older and there's a new generation of mass communication media theorists? Whenever the Global Communication Association has its meetings in San Francisco, a huge number of people always come. And it's mid-July, when the weather's generally decent, too.

"The academic world is divided into two groups of people: the somebodies, those who have made important contributions—like myself—who are looked at and listened to, and then there are all the others, those who are nobodies, like most of the people here, who do the looking and the listening. The somebodies are those who are looked at and

1

the nobodies are those who do the looking. The somebodies teach at the best universities. They do the research, write the important papers and books, and travel all over the world giving talks and appearing at one another's conferences and publishing one another's papers in their journals and books in their series while the nobodies, for the most part, teach what the somebodies, like myself, write. Just as well. I like to travel, and it's nice being able to pick up some travel funds from the dean or from academic organizations for my efforts."

He was sitting behind a long table. To his left was Mikhaila Blotnik-Kiev Vološinova. "She seems to get more beautiful every year," he thought. "And next to her is that jerk Nigel Haddley-Lassiter." Elijah recalled a conversation he'd had some years ago with Haddley-Lassiter, who prided himself on being an astute critic who could tear articles and books apart and show their methodological weaknesses. At the time Haddley-Lassiter hadn't published anything, and he was some thirty years younger than Ashdod-Sfard.

"You've rushed into print too soon," Haddley-Lassiter said, in a smug, self-important manner. "Actually, Elijah, your books are all unpublishable. You've only published those ten books of yours because you've somehow tricked editors!"

"If you're so smart, why haven't you published anything?" Ashdod-Sfard replied.

"My work," said Haddley-Lassiter, "is too good to published."

"What a schmuck Haddley-Lassiter is," thought Ashdod-Sfard. "He was a schmuck then and he's still one. All he's done for the most part is write one decent book and edit moronic readers and that kind of thing."

Elijah then glanced to his right. "There's Lisa Shauber Gurke," he thought, "who has taken her theory of media events and leveraged it into a professorship at the University of East Berlin and countless invitations to lecture at universities all over the world. She hasn't done anything in ages. Next to her is Jean-Georg Simmul, the latest big thing for the past twenty years in the intellectual world from France. Everyone on the panel is here.

"Simmul, at least, is smart," Elijah thought. "The French system puts out superstars, one after the other. It must be their system of education, because Frenchmen are not, genetically speaking, smarter than Israelis or Americans. The French are so arrogant, though. He's been very cold to me, in recent years. If looks could kill, I wouldn't be around very long. I wonder why he feels that way? I hope he didn't find out what I said about him when we were at that conference at Harvard last year."

More people came in. Now Elijah noticed some people he had met in the course of his travels—professors at first-tier universities, who had that look people who have "made it" have, and professors from second-, third-, and fourth-tier schools, who either were desperately trying to move up or had decided to make the best of their situation and didn't think they were going anyplace. "They go to first-rate grad schools and then end up at second-rate places. It's a big shock. But they can still lead decent lives," Elijah thought, "and they don't have to pay a million dollars for their houses, the way people at Berkeley and Stanford do. You can lead a good life teaching at second-rate institutions."

The session didn't start for another ten minutes, not until eight o'clock, so people were chatting with one another, and others were coming in and sitting down, some strategically in the back of the room so they could leave easily if they got bored. It was dark and windy outside, and it had suddenly started storming. The lights flickered every once in a while.

He turned to Mikhaila. "You're looking more beautiful than ever," he said to her. "The older you get the better you look, whereas I . . . ."

"Come now," said Mikhaila, interrupting him and smiling. She was beautiful and knew it, and she wore tight-fitting clothes that emphasized her voluptuous body. She was very slender, around five foot eight, and was wearing a black turtleneck jersey with sequins, a gray microminiskirt, and light blue stockings. Her red hair was loose and hung down almost to her waist.

"Men . . . . With men, for me, it's their brains that count," she replied, coyly. "And you're certainly most handsomely endowed in *that* category, Elijah. You don't have to worry if your hair is getting a bit thin. It's what's under it that counts."

Elijah, like many balding men, grew his hair long on the sides and combed it over his bald spots. It made him look silly and vain. And even a bit devious.

"Poor thing, you look tired," she said. "Have you been getting enough sleep?"

Suddenly, Elijah found himself in Moscow, where he'd come to give a lecture, with Mikhaila. They were in a suite in the Kremlin, in a large room full of beautiful French furniture. There were luxurious Turkish rugs on the floor. On the walls, a painting of a severe looking Lenin looked down on them. They were sitting opposite one another at a small table, which was lit by a beautiful crystal chandelier that hung from the ceiling. On the table were many crystal goblets, pieces of silver utensils, and a large Limoges plate with a starched white napkin on it. There were golden salt shakers and pepper shakers, a golden butter dish, and a large bottle of Italian sparkling water. There was soft music playing, coming from a Bose system discreetly placed at one end of the room. It was Tchaikovsky's Eugen Onegin. He recognized the singers. It was the disk with Nicolai Ghaurov, Alexandrina Pendachanka, Lybomir Dyakovski, and Niko Isakov. "I actually prefer the version with Dmitri Hrostovsky," he thought. A roaring fire in a huge stone fireplace warmed them. Near the fireplace, five sleek Borzois were dozing. He glanced at the dogs. "They're handsome dogs," he said.

"Zey're names are Grekh, Stradanyie, Skuka, Toska, and Pozor," she replied. "Lovely dogs, but zey are a bit neurotic—like everyone in Russia." She was wearing a glittering diamond tiara, a diamond necklace, and a beautiful evening gown. A butler in tails and white gloves appeared, carrying a tray with vodka, Beluga caviar, and blini. He poured some vodka into their glasses and placed a frosted bottle of Absolut vodka on the table.

"I hate to say it, but Absolut iss better than Stoli or any vodka we make nowadays. But our caviar iss still beyond compare."

When they had finished the blini and the caviar, the butler appeared with a soup tureen, a bowl with sour cream in it, a plate with some black bread on it, and two bowls. He ladled out steaming hot borsht into the soup bowls, gave them to Elijah and Mikhaila, and then disappeared.

"This soup is delicious," said Elijah.

"Yes," she replied, smiling.

She buttered some bread.

"I love borsht and black bread," said Mikhaila. "It reminds me of my roots in mother Russia."

She put some sour cream in her borsht.

"Mmm," she said. "When I was a child, zis was my favorite treat. I couldn't eat such rich food in my twenties, when I was prima ballerina assoluta of the Moscow ballet and had to watch my weight. I lived for years on little more than water and dried crusts of bread.

"There are many things in my past you don't know about, I'm sure. I prefer ze more mature men for my friends now," she said softly. "All my husbands were many years older than me. Younger men may be more vigorous, but I find zem to be terribly shallow and thin. There's no substance there. Zey have no ideas, only ambition.

That's why I like you. Some people think I'm looking for a father figure, since my father died when I was young. That may be. But that's not why I like you. I admire your brilliance, your worldliness, your wit. A good sense of humor iss important to me," she added. "And you have zhat rare ability to amuse me. Few men have. Unlike the members of the silent majorities you write about, I make my views known."

The butler appeared and took away their plates. Then he reappeared with two plates with pelmenyi in a cream sauce.

"Delicious," said Ashdod-Sfard. "I never thought Russian food could be so refined and taste so good."

The butler returned with another course. This one, coulibiec, featured salmon in flaky pastry that was served with a light dill sauce.

"Fabulous meal," said Ashdod-Sfard. "Absolutely superb."

Mikhaila took a small silver bell and rang it. The butler appeared.

"Sviatislav, we're ready for the main course now."

"Very good, madam," he said bowing. He took their empty plates and then he left.

"We Russians, you have to understand, dear Elijah, are strange people. We alternate between asceticism and orgiastic behavior. You see, we are swaddled when we are infants, and this swaddling leads, so psychologists tell us, to intense and destructive rage in us that generates fantasies of biting and destroying by devouring. We alternate between restraint without gratifications, when we are swaddled, and gratifications without restraint, when we are unswaddled and when we grow older. We then bear the burden of a transcendent sense of shame that becomes superimposed on a more archaic and diffuse sense of guilt. What we Russians value are not minimum gratifications—enough to get along with—but maximum total gratifications—orgiastic feasts, prolonged drinking bouts, and—I'm sure you'll be interested in zhis—a high frequency of copulation.

"Nearly all Russians," she continued, "would prefer a huge feast, followed by months of meager fare, rather than a little improvement in our daily diet. Russian men, alas, tend to be gross, coarse, lustful, and inconsiderate, which is why women like me, who come from families that are refined, sensitive, and spiritual, are attracted to men like you. So we Russians all carry around a diffuse sense of guilt in our unconscious and a diffuse feeling of fear. Everyone is a potential enemy. We are all lost in a gigantic country and we are plagued by boredom and by guilt. We are all unconsciously searching for absolution. It is a terrible burden.

"After dinner, I will repair to my private chapel for a brief moment where I will receive absolution from a holy father, Zossima Nikolaevich Medvedev, rector of the Ivanov Brethren confraternity. Then I will return to you, and we will take a walk in *the garden and discuss philosophical problems Perhaps you might even know some secrets I might be interested in?" She laughed.*

Then, suddenly, her eyes welled up, and she took a dainty handkerchief and wiped the tears away. The butler then appeared with a huge silver tray. On it was a small roast lamb, surrounded by roast potatoes and pickled red cabbage. Elijah could smell the garlic the chef had used on the lamb. Suddenly the chef, a big, fat man, appeared and started sharpening a long knife against a sharpening stone.

"It looks delicious, Mischa," said Mikhaila. It was obvious that her spirits had started to rise again.

"For you, madam," said Mischa, smiling, "I would do anything! Anything! You know that!"

He then sliced two portions of the lamb and put them on our plates, along with some roast potato and pickled red cabbage. He put a plate before each of us and then left. The lamb was delicious. The crust was crispy and the meat was light pink. It had been cooked to perfection. They ate hungrily. After they finished the main course, the butler appeared with some glasses held in silver containers, a pot of black tea, and some sweet cakes filled with honeyed poppy seeds. He poured the tea and put some cakes on their plates.

"A toast," said Mikhaila, filling Elijah's glass with more vodka. "To our friendship."

Elijah was getting full and the vodka he'd been drinking was slowly getting to his head. He felt a bit dizzy.

"I could use a nice nap now," he thought. "I like to sleep for a while after a big meal." Mikhaila was absolutely radiant. Her beauty astounded Elijah. Her eyes were sparkling and her hair glowed brilliantly in the soft light. Suddenly her image started getting blurred, and then it started fading away. In a few seconds she had disappeared.

"Um . . . um . . . what did you say?" said Elijah. "I'm afraid my mind must have wandered a bit. I was thinking about my introduction to the session that will be starting shortly."

"I asked you if you're getting enough sleep," she repeated.

"Oh, . . . oh, yes, thank you." At that moment, for reasons he couldn't quite fathom, he felt a bit depressed.

She leaned close to him, and he could smell her perfume. She bent over and whispered into his ear, "I know that you're really a dirty old man!" Then she laughed and pinched him on the cheek.

On his right, Lisa Shauber Gurke was sitting, chatting to someone from the audience who had come over to talk with her. She was talking in German to a tall man whose name tag indicated he was a professor at some German technical university. He was laughing at something she said. She looked pale and very fragile, and she was coughing weakly. Her glasses, he noticed, had small hearing aids on them. That was new—he had never seen her with them before. She was short and emaciated, with gray hair that she wore pulled tightly behind her. She had long, silver earrings and was wearing a necklace that looked like it had come from one of those Indian tribes in New Mexico.

"Probably she's saying something insulting about Americans," Elijah thought. "And Israelis, as well. She's a real bitch."

He looked at all the people sitting behind the table. "Hmm," he thought. "Actually, if you think about it, most of my colleagues sitting with me can't stand one another. They may actually hate one another. They also have colossal egos, because of some overpraised book or stupid theory they developed. Most of them haven't done anything to speak of for years, maybe decades.

"Lisa hates Mikhaila because she's such a knockout and is so popular, and Mikhaila hates Lisa because she prevented Mikhaila from getting a juicy position at Harvard. Lisa was a referee and wrote a poisonous evaluation of Mikhaila's work. What Lisa wrote about Mikhaila was nothing compared to what Lisa's written about Simmul. She positively loathes him. I wonder why? Maybe they were an item once and he dumped her? Maybe she resents his arrogance? Maybe she hates Frenchmen? Maybe it has something to do with his being connected with the Deuxième Bureau, if the rumors about him are true? Something must have gone on between them. And since my negative review of Simmul's latest book, there's even more bad blood between us, too. He's become very angry and bitter in recent years, and he doesn't let go of his grudges. He probably recognizes that he's slipping. I wonder if his mind's going on him?"

"Sorry to interrupt your little lovefest with Mikhaila," said Lisa snidely, tapping Elijah on the shoulder. "I'm not feeling well and need to go back to my room to take some medicine. So please start without me. I should be back in five or ten minutes."

"I'm terribly sorry," said Elijah, feigning concern. "By all means. We'll start without you; when you're feeling better, come right back. Your seat will be waiting for you. Everyone wants to hear what you have to say, that's for certain. You're probably the reason most people are here at this session, instead of lingering over dinner."

"You're most kind," she replied, but he could see she didn't mean it. She looked at Elijah with an icy, rather hateful stare. Then she got up and walked away from the table with slow, hesitant steps and left the room. The tall man was with her, holding her arm, as if to support her.

Haddley-Lassiter was sitting next to Mikhaila, and they were chatting softly.

"How ironic," thought Elijah. "I'm at the same table with that insufferable Haddley-Lassiter. Fortunately, Mikhaila is sitting between us. I have no use for him." His eyes narrowed when he looked at Haddley-Lassiter, and there was, for a brief moments, a look of hatred reflected in those eyes.

"I'd better be on good behavior tonight," Elijah thought. "Otherwise I won't get invited to chair panels at conferences or give lectures any more. No sense in dwelling on the past and letting it destroy you."

He turned to his right. Jean-Georg Simmul was looking over his notes, getting prepared, no doubt, to launch yet another intellectual bombshell for the benefit of the Global Communication Association and the scholarly world.

"He does have a fantastic imagination," thought Elijah, "and the remarkable ability to stay three steps ahead of everyone during a discussion of almost any topic. I wonder how he does it? Maybe he should be seen as a fiction writer and not a sociologist—or whatever he is."

Simmul looked out over the audience. "I've got to go through yet another one of these boring and moronic panel discussions," he thought. "And they put me next to that monster Lisa, too. She hates me and has written terrible things about me. But who hasn't? Not that it matters—they're all jealous. Why couldn't they have put me next to Mikhaila? She's beautiful and she has brains, too. And she's pleasant. Just the kind of woman I like."

Elijah glanced around the room. People were still coming in. "I'll wait a few minutes more," he thought. "There's no hurry."

"We'll wait a few more minutes, if you don't mind," he said to his colleagues on the panel. "People are still coming in."

Lisa came back in the room and took her place behind the table.

"I'm feeling much better now," she said. "I see the panel hasn't started yet, so I didn't miss anything. That's good."

"No, we haven't started yet but will in a couple of minutes. Jean-

Georg will be our first speaker, then you, Lisa. Then Mikhaila will give her presentation, and Nigel will be the last speaker."

Elijah looked at his notes. He was in a most familiar role—as moderator of a panel. For many years he had traveled all over the world doing the same thing, though he did give lectures occasionally. This time the panel was on mass communication theory. The year before at the conference in London he had chaired one on audiences. And next year? It would be in Paris.

"I certainly don't want to miss the conference in Paris, whatever it will be on," he thought. "Even though we will be in Jean-Georg's territory."

He took another look at the audience. Just a few stragglers were coming in, and the audience had started to settle down.

"Time to start," he thought. He stood up.

"Ladies and gentlemen," he said. "I'd like to welcome you to this panel on 'New Developments in Mass Communication Theory.' We have an outstanding panel of speakers here, as any of you familiar with mass communication theory know. For those of you who know their names but don't know what they look like, let me introduce the members of my panel. On my far left, we have Nigel Haddley-Lassiter, from the London School of Economics. His brilliant book X-Effects has caused a big stir in our field. Next to him, on my immediate left, is Mikhaila Blotnik-Kiev Vološinova, whose latest book, Conversationalism: The Importance of Dialogue in Communication, is required reading. My name is Elijah Ashdod-Sfard, and I assume, and hope, that some of you know my work—The Cycle of Silence or some of my other books. On my right, physically and perhaps politically as well, is Lisa Schauber Gurke, whose book The Meaning of Media Events is probably known to all of you. And finally, next to Lisa, we find Jean-Georg Simmul, father of the semiotic theory of hyperreality and author of The System of Things and more than a dozen other books on media, postmodernism, and related topics.

"He will be our first speaker. With great pleasure I introduce my dear friend and esteemed colleague, professor Jean-Georg Simmul of the University of Paris X. He will speak on 'The Evangelical Hamburger,' whose title is enigmatic and intriguing and, dare I say it, one that sounds very meaty."

The people in the audience applauded.

McLuhan became frustrated trying to teach first year students in required courses how to read English poetry, and began using the technique of analysing the front page of newspapers, comic strips, ads, and the like as poems—applying the new critical techniques he had encountered in the Cambridge school as interpreted through his sense of the history of literature and rhetorical expression and expressed in a histrionic stance reinforced by his natural wit. This new approach to the study of popular culture and popular art forms led to his first major move towards new media and communication and eventually resulted in his first book, *The Mechanical Bride*, which some consider to be one of the founding documents of early cultural studies. While the *Bride* was not initially a success, it introduced one aspect of McLuhan's basic method—using poetic methods of analysis in a quasi poetic style to analyse popular culture phenomena. . . . [T]he *Bride* illustrated yet another aspect of the ongoing McLuhanesque approach to cultural phenomena—the satiric use of wit and the comic as a mode of "tweaking" hidden levels of meaning and complexity from material that seems to be relatively simple—*Blondie, Li'l Abner,* the front page of a Hearst tabloid, ads for caskets, laundry soap, or stockings.

—Donald F. Theall, *The Virtual Marshall McLuhan*, pp. 4, 5

2

The Evangelical Hamburger

Jean-Georg Simmul smiled. He waited for a minute while his mind cleared itself. He turned on the microphone that was in front of him.

"Thank you so much for that most kind introduction, Elijah. It's a distinct pleasure as well as a great honor to be on this panel with such distinguished scholars, people who have contributed so much to the study of communication, which has emerged, if I may be so bold, as the primary concern of current scholarship since it is, we now recognize, so central to everything. Our focus here, of course, is on mass communication—in contrast to those who study interpersonal communication or organizational communication or any other kind of communication.

"And what do the empiricists tell us about communication? I find most interesting a famous pronouncement made some sixty years ago by Bernard Berelson. What did he tell us? That some kind of *communication* on some kinds of *issues*, brought to the attention of some kinds of *people* under some kinds of *conditions*, have some kinds of *effects*. Perhaps true, but not very edifying or encouraging to those of us who think there may be more to the matter of analyzing media and communication and mass culture than this—especially American culture and society.

"I must confess that I always love coming to America. I love the desert; I like the giant cities; I like the fact that here in America people will, at least, listen to me without attacking every other word I speak or write, which is the situation in Europe. Perhaps it is because Americans are the most postmodern of all people, with their shopping malls, with Las Vegas, with their remarkable architects, with their hip-hoppers and teenyboppers, with all the fabulous crazies that inhabit this country. I like the fast-food joints; the football games; the hideous, stultifying boredom of the suburbs. Postmodernism argues that the old philosophical abstractions and absolutes no longer work and that we should see the world in terms of irony, depthlessness, the dissolution of the difference between elite and popular culture, the eclectic mixture of aesthetic elements and that kind of thing.

"America is the land of seduction, of a new approach to things that breaks with the referentiality of sex and provides a space, not for desire, but for play and defiance. It is for this reason I find the critique of the feminists about phallic power so *lacking*—a word that is fraught with peril, I recognize, when dealing with sexuality and feminism. My focus on play and desires offers an insight into things, and one that is not as simplistic as the traditional feminist one, reducing sexual relations to one dimension—a biological one that is connected, so they believe, to dominance and subservience."

"Oh, my God," thought Lisa Schauber Gurke, "He's at it again. He's getting worse and worse. I think his mind is really beginning to go on him. I was broken-hearted when our affair ended twenty years ago, but now I'm glad it did. How I could ever have been attracted to that man is beyond me." She shuddered; then she glanced at her watch nervously and drummed her fingers softly on the table.

"America is the land of the hyperreal," Simmul continued, "where everything is a simulation of something that is in turn a simulation of something that is not real. How do we find the real when we are immersed in the hyperreal, in simulations that reflect upon themselves, until, like a person in a hall of mirrors, we find ourselves looking at reflections of reflections that repeat themselves endlessly?"

"He hasn't had a new idea in thirty years," thought Mikhaila Blotnik-Kiev Vološinova. "He's not really serious. That's a problem with those

French scholars. You never know when they are putting you on. If I hear his nonsense about hamburgers one more time, I'll scream. Or vomit."

"It is when we recognize," Simmul added, "that the everyday objects that surround us can be looked at as signs and thus as peepholes into the society and culture that generates them that we can start to make sense of the objects that play such an important role in our everyday lives. Our urban civilization is witness to an ever-accelerating procession of generations of products, appliances, and gadgets by comparison with which mankind appears to be a remarkably stable species. Some questions we must consider: how are objects experienced, what needs other than functional ones do they answer, what mental structures are interwoven with—and contradict—their functional structures?

"There is all around us today a kind of fantastic consciousness of consumption and abundance, constituted by the multiplication of objects, services and material goods, and this represents something of a fundamental mutation in the ecology of the human species. Strictly speaking, the humans of the age of affluence are surrounded not so much by other human beings, as they were in previous ages, but by objects.

"We must remember that every object or property is an extension of our personality; property is that which obeys our wills, that in which our egos express and externally realize themselves. This expression occurs, earliest and most completely, in regard to our body, which is our first and most unconditional possession. We are, in a sense, our things. The objects that surround us do not simply have utilitarian aspects; rather they serve as a kind of mirror that reflects our own image. Objects surrounding us permit us to discover more and more aspects of ourselves. In a sense, therefore, a knowledge of the soul of things is possibly a direct and new and revolutionary way of discovering the soul of man.

"We must place these objects, of course, within the new system of consumption that structures our desires. There is, in modern capitalist consumption cultures, an ethic of consumption, a need to consume—and to consume endlessly. The consumer is, in one sense, a patriot who keeps things going, who feeds the engine of democracy, who ensures that there will be work for people, who will produce what others consume and consume what others produce. In another sense, the consumer is devastating the planet.

"With this in mind, let me offer a reprise, in a revised and updated form, in many places, on some speculations about various phenomena of life that I have put forth earlier in various places and that are, I believe—and I hope you will agree with me—still worth considering. I will start with my thoughts about McDonald's hamburgers and what I call 'the evangelical hamburger.' "

THE EVANGELICAL HAMBURGER

"I had explained, many years ago, that McDonald's was an 'evangelical hamburger' that would eventually spread its golden arches all over the world, deluding people into thinking, by a process I called 'hambour-geoisment,' that their access to cheap ground meat meant they were middle class. (That is, I argued, the dynamics of the McDonald's organization and their numerous outlets resembled the dynamics of evangelical religions.)

"We know, now, that I was correct. McDonald's is now everywhere, functioning as a symbol of an American 'with-it' attitude in foreign countries all over the world. I was talking with a young child in France recently and mentioned that I was going to America where I would have a McDonald's hamburger.

" 'Do they have them there?' asked the child. 'I thought we only had them in France!' "

"Very cute, very cute, indeed," thought Nigel Haddley-Lassiter. "I think it's his style, his opaqueness, his use of paradox, his seeming seriousness, when he's really laughing at all of us, that is the key to his popularity. Why people can't see through his nonsense is beyond me. I believe in the British and American empirical tradition—do research, conduct experiments, and let the data speak for itself. These Europeans, with their philosophical approach to communication, with their obscure postmodern theories and semiotic nonsense. For them, and especially for scholars like Simmul, anything goes."

MOTELIZATION THEORY

"I also elaborated a theory of 'motelization' in the early seventies," Simmul continued. "In an article on the subject I suggested that the American household was becoming like a motel, with the family unit more or less decomposing and disappearing (I admit that I'm exaggerating things a bit here, as is my nature). I argued that family members had become too absorbed in their own personal activities and had weakened if not severed their sense of connection, loyalty, or responsibility toward others in their families and toward others in their societies. In motelized families, thanks to changes in the design of houses, young men and women had direct access from their cars to their bedrooms, just like in motels.

"These self-absorbed people seldom appeared in the kitchen, except when they were hungry and, after 'raiding' the refrigerator, zapped things in the microwave, gobbled their food down and went off to their rooms and later on to their adventures. They ate alone, and as a recent sociologist has argued, they now bowl alone.

"There were, I explained, some advantages to this arrangement. Children would no longer find it necessary to run away from home to take drugs and have sex since they would now have direct access to their own bedrooms. The parents, in this 'mom and pop' form of family/ motel, would take care of the laundry and provide food for meals. An ideal arrangement as far as disaffected children were concerned—and one that seems to be, more and more, the norm.

"And now let me turn to muscle cars—a subject of compelling interest, I must say. We must always keep in mind the so-called love affair of Americans with their cars."

MUSCLE CARS AND DEFLOWERING AND THE SEXUAL
IDENTITY OF APPLIANCES

"I have also suggested that television commercials showing 'muscle' cars crashing through roadside signs and similar barriers represented, symbolically, the deflowering of virgins! We are not talking about seduction here, either.

"In the same vein, I have argued that household appliances had genders and could be classified according to their sexual identities. (After all, most appliances, if you think about it, are receptacles and womblike, reflecting what has been described as the 'incorporative modality.' The only significant household male electric appliances with the 'penetrating modality' that I could find were electric knives, hand blenders, hedge trimmers and leaf blowers.) Tools, of course, are often hyperphallic, but they aren't household appliances. One important appliance that deserves investigation, of course, is the freezer."

INFANTILE STARVATION AND THE PURCHASE
OF FREEZERS

"Speaking of appliances, I have also suggested that there might be a
correlation between infantile hunger and, when these infants who have
starved grow up and get older, the purchase of huge freezers, which
they fill with enormous amounts of food—even though there are supermarkets, open twenty-four hours, all over the place in America. This
hunger, I deduced, was caused by parents who read books about babies
being 'spoiled' if they were fed off schedule. This is no longer held to
be a good idea, but at one time it was thought to be proper. We are, in
effect, little machines, so the books on raising children argued, and if
parents fed their babies whenever they wanted to eat, when they were
hungry, these parents would be harming their children.

"So the parents, trying to do the right thing, let their babies, who
might not have had a good feeding and were hungry, cry between feed-
ings, until they passed out from starvation and exhaustion. But they
remembered, down deep in their psyches, what it was like to be starv-
ing. In later years, when they could afford them, they purchased huge
freezers and stuffed them with food."

PHILOSOPHICAL PERSPECTIVES: I STINK
THEREFORE I AM AND TO BUY IS TO BE PERCEIVED

"I had written an article about deodorants with a whimsical title, 'I Stink,
Therefore I Am,' suggesting that the American passion to remove body
odor was tied, ultimately, to Puritanism, perfectionism, and a fear of
death. Body odor is not a problem for people in France, in part, because
we do not believe we can be perfect, like the Americans do.

"In the same vein, I had speculated, in an essay called 'To Buy Is To
Be Perceived' (playing upon Bishop Berkeley's famous dictum 'to be is
to be perceived'), that most of us lead lives, not only of 'quiet desperation,' as Thoreau put it, but also of relative anonymity. Generally speaking, it is only when we purchase things that anyone pays (notice the
term) much attention to us. And when they do, it is only pro forma. We
get few personal letters nowadays, and we need the bills in the mail to
remind ourselves (prove to ourselves?) that we do, in fact, exist. The
consumer society becomes, then, an attempt to assuage the alienation
generated by the American bourgeois economic system."

WHITE (BALLOON) BREAD AND LACK OF IDEOLOGY IN AMERICA

"I had also hypothesized, in an article in *Tel Quel*, that traditional white or American balloon bread reflected a lack of ideology in America, where political parties, unlike European ideological parties, often compromise on important issues. There was a curious correspondence, I continued, between countries that liked bread with hard crusts (such as our wonderful French bread) and ideological thinking.

"American balloon bread, which has a very soft crust, can be squeezed into a small ball and manipulated into any shape desired. Just like many American politicians. The fact that nowadays there is a revolution in American bread and they are getting hard-crusted breads in many American bakeries and stores reflects, I suggest, the fact that American politics is also getting more ideological. The amazing recent popularity of bagels is something to which, I believe, political scientists should pay a good deal of attention."

STATUS IN FOODS OR DINING IN THE BEST CIRCLES

"A number of years ago a book was published in London listing cheap places to eat; the criterion was, to put it bluntly, how much food for how little cost. Its title, *Fuel Food*, captures an attitude toward food that many people in England and America have—or had, since tastes change, and now London is reputed to have many excellent restaurants. Food is fuel for the body machine, and food's basic function is to keep us going, so we can work hard, play hard, and do whatever it is we care to do.

"From this point of view, eating is not a source of sensual pleasure and delight but is, instead, functional and obligatory. This notion is, I would suggest, a residue of ascetic Protestantism, which has shaped American minds to a great extent and now, we discover, their bodies. The attitudes of Americans have been influenced by their Puritan heritage, which has not only affected their sexuality but also their food preferences. There is a question now as to how powerful Puritanism is in contemporary America and the degree to which its influence is ebbing. In the contemporary postmodern society, Puritanism doesn't seem to make much of an impact on young, and now increasingly older, people's behavior.

"In a remarkable essay called 'Gastrosophy: The Philosophy of Food,' the celebrated Mexican poet and writer Octavio Paz investigated this matter of food preferences and came to some fascinating conclusions. The adjectives he uses to describe American food tell his story. American cuisine, he says, is simple, spiceless, honest, and based on exclusions, just like American culture. American food 'ignores ambiguity and ambivalence,' and American beverages such as gin and whiskey accentuate 'withdrawal' and 'unsociability.'

"Paz compares American food with Mexican and French food, both of which he says involve blendings, transubstantiations, and mysteries. Compared to these cuisines, American food, with its emphasis on purity and passion for milk and ice cream—that is, pregenital innocence—is rather tasteless and bland.

"We might say that in America dining *has been replaced by eating*. Instead of meals being socializing experiences and happy occasions, large numbers of people tend to look on meals as interruptions in their daily lives. There are millions of families who hardly ever eat a meal together; people grab what they can in passing, and nobody in the family sees one another, around the dining room table or anyplace else, for that matter. I have already alluded to this in my discussion of 'motelization.' We know of very primitive peoples that they do not eat at set times but rather anarchically—eating individually whenever each person gets hungry. Perhaps we are moving in that direction now?

"The whole fast-food industry represents, if you think about it, an attitude toward food; the mechanization and technologizing of food has a grimness and alienating quality about it that is profoundly disturbing to many people. On the other hand, there is now in the United States an increasing interest in gourmet cooking, but this has been limited, it seems, to relatively small, educated, 'sophisticated' elements in the population. As Americans travel more, their taste and sophistication in matters pertaining to food is changing. We see this in the growth of excellent restaurants and in the acceptance of espresso coffee.

"Attitudes toward food, we must remember, are essentially cultural. English food is, or used to be—and probably still is, as a rule—undistinguished, though London now has many first-class restaurants; eating seems to be unimportant to the English, while twelve miles across the channel, we French seem to have made eating one of the focal points of our lives. Statistics show that people in France used to spend more time eating—an average of 106 minutes a day—than anyone else. They also used to spend a lot of time sleeping—time spent sleeping correlates with time spent eating—leading some to describe the French as having an 'eat-sleep' culture. This is changing in recent years as fast food has, alas, become popular in France.

"Although we seldom think about it, we all carry around in our heads attitudes and beliefs about food that determine how and what we eat. We all have certain codes and principles of organization that we use when we plan a meal. That is what a cuisine is. We pick up, though we are unaware of it, preferences and rules of combination that affect what we eat. For example, though the English eat great quantities of Brussels sprouts and carrots and fried fish, you do not see 'Fish and Sprouts' shops or 'Fish and Carrots' shops because we all know, having been taught so, that chips go with fish and nothing else. Americans seldom eat boiled potatoes with steak and never boil steak—though it is possible to boil steak, it is inconceivable. Why? Because it violates their codes about what is proper to do with fresh red meat that is tender enough to broil or grill.

"Different foods and different kinds of foods have different statuses. When people are invited out to dinner, it is not unusual for them to speculate about what will be served. I know I generally do this. The reason we do so is to determine how highly our company is valued by our hosts, how much esteem we are to be granted.

"Generally speaking, I would suggest the following chart compares high- and low-status foods in America."

High-Status Foods	Low-Status Foods
Roast beef	Hamburger
Steak	Stews
Duck	Chicken

STATUS OF FOODS IN AMERICA

"According to this scheme, roast beef and steak have very high ratings, while stews and hamburger dishes have relatively low status, and duck or pheasant, being uncommon, has more status than chicken. When gourmet cooking is involved, the ranking system doesn't work perfectly because we have now introduced a foreign element into our considerations—veal. Veal, which is highly regarded in Europe, is not generally esteemed as highly here. If you serve your guests a dish using veal, they will find it difficult to estimate what you think of them. Veal confounds in America.

"We can also make a distinction between everyday food and gourmet *special occasions* food.

Everyday	Gourmet
Easy to prepare	Hard to prepare
Inexpensive	Expensive
Routine	Special occasion
American	Foreign (often)
Soda pop	Wine
Early evening	Late evening

"Americans don't eat gourmet meals very often, because they are expensive and take a great deal of time to prepare. A friend of mine told me that he and his wife have taken to eating out a great deal because his wife only likes to cook gourmet dinners, and it takes so much time and effort to prepare these meals that they end up going to modest restaurants many evenings. This after they spent thirty or forty thousand dollars remodeling their kitchen.

"This matter of deciding the status of meals is frequently taken care of for us in restaurants; there the price of the items gives it its status, and what you order gives you your status in the waiter's mind. In fancy restaurants where waiters are often tyrants and snobs, a great deal of pressure is exerted on us to order expensive dishes and prove that we belong. Unfortunately, as many of us from France, and Europe, as well, keep finding out, in gourmet restaurants in America, we tend to consume style rather than superb food.

"Although food is one of those subjects most people tend to take for granted, it is a subject of immense importance. Anthropologists have been engaged in food research for many years, and many are now involved with 'deciphering' meals, analyzing them in terms of their principles of organization and not in terms of kinds of foods served. Thus, meals can be studied in terms of their constituent elements—sours and sweets, solids and liquids, hards and softs, raw food and cooked food— and the way these elements are combined. From this point of view, the traditional meal of roast beef, roast potatoes, and peas is a study in circles of varying diameters. I assume here that one is not a dot-com millionaire who can afford a standing rib roast.

"If you think food is important, you must look at the supermarket in an entirely different way. It is not a store but rather a mass medium of staggering cultural significance. It 'broadcasts' food in the same manner that McDonald's, Burger King, Jack in the Box, and Taco Bell 'broadcast' fast meals. The fact that both the supermarkets and fast-food joints are broadcasting so much hamburger has great significance. Here we find the digestive system and the socioeconomic system meeting in the hamburger system. Isn't it remarkable what you sometimes can find in chopped meat?"

HUMOR AND CRIMINALITY: A MODEST PROPOSAL THAT
NEVER GOT MADE

"At the beginning of my academic career, when I was full of high seriousness, which is common for young scholars, I had an idea for doing some important research. I found a colleague who, along with me, was interested in investigating whether criminals have a different sense of humor from noncriminals. We applied for a grant for one million francs, with me as principal investigator, to test this hypothesis but, tragically, were turned down. We wanted to find out whether criminals had a different sense of humor from noncriminals to further knowledge, for essentially intellectual reasons, one might say. I had thought it would be good to do a multicultural study, testing criminals not only in Paris but also in America—in New York, San Francisco, New Orleans, and Miami Beach.

"I had a modest proposal to make, which, alas, never got made. I reasoned as follows. If we discover that criminals do, in fact, have a different sense of humor than noncriminals, we can develop a humor test, an instrument, that would allow us to identify or discover not only who are and who are not criminals but also, more important, who will be criminals.

"We could give this test to children and adolescents, and if they showed criminality in their sense of humor, I reasoned, we could throw them in jail *before* they committed their crimes. This would save people, I suggested, from the terrible feelings of anguish and violation they suffer when mugged or robbed and from the loss of money and property from burglaries and other crimes.

"This Criminal Sense of Humor Instrument would also have saved the taxpayers a considerable amount of money, wasted generally, on programs by psychologists and social workers for disturbed and criminal youth. When, if ever, problem youth or career criminals tested negatively on the criminal sense of humor test, we could let them go, with little fear of recidivism."

NEW PROJECTS

"I would like to say a few words about what I'm doing now. As many of you know, I have more or less renounced the printed word in favor of the photographic image. In an age of simulations, what is more real than the unreality of the photographic image. There is something about the photograph that has fascinated semioticians and many other scholars in recent years, and the reason for this, I would suggest, is that the photograph is the ne plus ultra of simulation. The world is not real anymore, as I have explained countless times, but the photograph is real. In an era of simulations, signifiers are more real than their signifieds and it is the photograph, that real image of an imaginary reality, to which we must turn to find our way.

"Let me conclude by suggesting that in the contemporary world of hyperreality and supersimulation, what you see is frequently not what you get, and what you get quite often is not what you see. Seeing is believing, so we are told, but all too often because what we see is unreal these beliefs are false. The imagination is now more the key to reality than the senses. That is why the commercial for the McDonald's hamburger is infinitely more satisfying than the hamburger itself! And less fattening, too, I might add.

"I thank you for your kind attention."

With that Jean-Georg took a drink of water and put his notes into a manila folder. There was a loud round of applause from the members of the audience, some of whom stood up and shouted "Bravo, bravo," and the members of the panel also politely applauded. The people who were standing sat down after a couple of minutes. Several people in the audience raised their hands, so they could ask questions.

"Thank you, Jean-Georg," said Elijah Ashdod-Sfard, "for another one of your brilliant inquiries, full of your remarkable insights. It was a presentation, I have no reservation in saying, that only you could have delivered."

"Or only you would have wanted to deliver," Ashdod-Sfard thought. He continued, "I see that some people in the audience have questions. Let me ask you to save all your questions until everyone in the panel has spoken. Then we will have a decent amount of time to ask questions of all the panelists. And now, we move to the second speaker . . . ."

At that moment, the lights in the room suddenly went out.

"What's happening?" people in the audience asked. "What's going on? Is it the storm, or was there a short circuit?" Various people in the audience continued to call out, "Someone do something! Open the door to the hallway!" During the chaos, someone uttered a very soft moan. Another person yelled "ouch," as he banged into a chair.

Suddenly, perhaps three or four minutes after the lights had gone off, the lights went on again. Jean-Georg Simmul was bent over, with his head resting on the table, and a silver stiletto was sticking out of his back. The material on his jacket around the knife was stained dark red from blood.

"Good Lord!" cried Elijah. "Someone's murdered Jean-Georg Simmul!" There were cries of anguish from people in the audience.

"Get the police!" a woman screamed.

"Yes, the police," said someone else.

Lisa Shauber Gurke looked like she was going to faint. Mikhaila Blotnik-Kiev Vološinova had turned a ghastly white. Nigel Haddley-Lassiter was wiping sweat from his forehead and neck and seemed to be having trouble breathing.

Someone in the audience had used a cell phone to call 911 and was transferred to the police to tell them what happened.

"The police will be here shortly," he announced. "They've asked that nobody leave the room until they've arrived."

Other people in the room were using their cell phones to spread the news.

"We'll all wait here until the police come," said Elijah Ashdod-Sfard, weakly. This has been a terrible tragedy." He had a pained look on his face.

We must replace emotional speculation with valid evidence as a basis for public discussion about mass communication. The different media have variously been charged with responsibility for (1) lowering the public's cultural tastes, (2) increasing rates of delinquency, (3) contributing to general moral deterioration, (4) lulling the masses into political superficiality, and (5) suppressing creativity. This is a damning list, and if the apparently innocent devices are actually guilty of such monstrous influences they should, of course, be viewed with alarm. The problem is that advocates of opposite points of view tell us that our newspapers, radios, television sets, and the like, are not insidious devices for evil but are in fact our faithful servants or even saviors in that they are (1) exposing sin and corruption, (2) acting as guardians of precious free speech, (3) bringing at least some culture to millions, (4) providing harmless entertainment for the tired masses of the labor force, (5) informing us of world's events, and (6) making more bountiful our standard of living by their unrelenting insistence that we purchase and consume products to stimulate our economic institution.

—Melvin L. DeFleur and Sandra Ball-Rokeach, *Theories of Mass Communication,* 4th ed., p. 1

"I'm Inspector
Solomon Hunter,"
said the man in the
tweed Brooks
Brothers suit . . .

"I'm Inspector Solomon Hunter," said the man in the tweed Brooks Brothers suit, as he walked in the door. He was a man of about sixty, with graying auburn hair, horn rim glasses that were tinted light gray, and eyes that moved around the room, taking in everything. He had the look of a college professor in some film from the fifties, when professors were seen as amusing fuddy-duddies, who weren't able to cope with the real world. "And this is my assistant, Sergeant Talcott Weems," he added, pointing to a tall, slightly stooped-over man in a tan poplin suit. He was bald and had a thin mustache. It had only taken five or six minutes for them to arrive, with a contingent of uniformed police officers.

Everyone in the room, in a state of shock, stared at the inspector. Hunter walked over to the body and looked at it carefully, as if he were taking a photograph of it and storing the photograph in his memory. Then he looked at the members of the panel who were sitting behind the table, near Simmul's body. Hunter looked at each of them, for an instant, almost as if they were specimens beneath a microscope.

"We're going to have someone from our unit talk with everyone in the room, briefly," he said, "but it is the people who were closest to the

25

dead man whom we're going to interrogate most closely. I'll be doing that right away."

"Weems," he said, turning to his assistant. "Have the coroner do an autopsy of the body. I want a report by tomorrow morning at the latest. Also, we'll need a couple of rooms, right away. We'll need a suite for the members of the panel to rest in and a room for us to carry out our interrogations. Get in touch with the manager and see what he can do for us. We'll need a tape recorder set up in the room where the interrogations will be held. And secure the professor's room. I want a twenty-four-hour guard on it, starting right away. I want to look around in it after we've finished with the members of the panel."

Men from the unit were taking photographs of Simmul. Others were dusting for fingerprints. Weems went out into the corridor and returned a couple of minutes later.

"I called the manager. The room's secured. It's locked and we'll have it guarded twenty-four hours a day with one of our men. We can have rooms 1007 and 1009, just down the hallway. He's sending someone up with the keys."

"Good," said Hunter. He turned to address the people in the room.

"I'm going to have one of my men interview every one of you in the audience. They'll want your name, where you're staying and that kind of thing. It's strictly routine, let me assure you. It doesn't mean that we suspect any of you. But maybe someone saw something that will be of use to us. Sometimes things that seem unimportant and trivial and not worth mentioning turn out to be very important to us, so please don't hold anything back.

"The victim was at the end of the table here, and someone from outside could have slipped in the door and killed him. There was, so I understand, chaos in the room for a few minutes, when the lights went out. Or . . . ," he paused for a few moments, "it also could have been someone already in the room, someone in the audience. And maybe even someone on the panel."

There was a sigh of astonishment from the people in the audience. The members of the panel glanced at one another with questioning looks and a touch of anxiety.

"Do you actually think the murderer could be one of us?" asked Ashdod-Sfard, with a tone of incredulity in his voice. "Are you suggesting

that one of *us* is a murderer? I have to say I find that idea quite preposterous. We're professors with international reputations. We don't go
around murdering people!"

Hunter said nothing, but there was a faint smile on his face. A policeman came in the room carrying two small plastic cards.

"Here are the card keys to get in the rooms," he said. He handed
them to Weems. The room was crowded with police officers taking photographs, videotaping the body of Jean-Georg Simmul and the members
of the panel who were seated near him.

"Those of you in the audience," said Hunter, "please stay here and
I'll have my men interview you right in this room. It won't take but a
minute or two. And you who are members of the panel," he said, glancing at them, "if you'll kindly follow Sergeant Weems, he will take you to
a suite where you can relax. There'll be a man at the door protecting
you. There's a killer loose, and he—or she—may try to kill again."

The members of the panel got up and followed Weems to the suite,
where they were to wait to be interrogated. The manager had sent up a
tray of coffee, juice, pastries, and sandwiches.

"I'll go and see what Inspector Hunter wants to do," said Weems to
the members of the panel. "I'll be back soon to tell you who he wants
to interrogate first. Meanwhile, you can relax and try to recall exactly
what happened before the lights went out and what you heard, if anything, after the lights went out."

He left the room and walked across the hallway to the room where
Solomon Hunter was getting ready to interrogate the members of the
panel. A policeman was setting up a tape recorder.

"They're in the suite," said Weems.

"Good," said Hunter. "Let them sit for a while."

"Do you think one of them did it?" asked Weems.

"Possibly. Maybe . . . even probably. But we'll see what we learn when
I start interviewing them. Meanwhile, get in touch with headquarters
and ask our intelligence unit to get whatever information it can on the
members of the panel. They're all listed on this program from the communications society."

He handed Weems a copy of the program.

"Have someone call their universities and get whatever they can
about each of them, including the victim. Have someone check their

names on the Internet. Also, all of these professors on the panel are from foreign countries. Have someone dig around with some of our associates overseas—Interpol or whatever—to find out what they can about them. I want all the biographical stuff we can get. From grade school on."

"What about the womb?" asked Weems. "Why stop at grade school?"

"If you can get it, Talcott," said Hunter, "that would be even better. The more we know, the better. These people are all, so I understand, famous scholars, who've been around a long time. You never can tell what you'll find when you start digging into their backgrounds. Any one of them, or more than one of them, might have killed Simmul. For any one of a thousand reasons. We've got one dead professor and four live ones from the panel, each of whom has to be considered a suspect."

"Who do you want to start with?" asked Weems.

"Let's start with the person farthest away from the victim. It was Had-dley-Lassiter, the professor who was sitting next to that really attractive red-headed woman. Send him in. And while you're at it, get me a chart with the names of each of the people in the panel, indicating where they were sitting. We know that Professor Simmul was at one end of the panel, and Haddley-Lassiter, if I remember correctly, was at the other end of the panel. I think he's a Brit. You know how Brits have these crazy names; sometimes they have four or five middle names."

He took a little notebook from a pocket in his jacket.

"Obviously British—his first name is Nigel. That's a very British name. He's at the London School of Economics. Let's see what he has to tell us."

"I've always found those British professors from the fancy universities to be impossible," said Weems. "They think they know everything, and, in addition, they think that they're better than everyone else. Like the Stanford professors around here. But the Brits usually went to all those fancy public schools and have lots of attitude. They're such snobs!"

"Don't make those generalizations," Talcott. "Your head is full of stereotypes and all kinds of other junk. You have to take people as you find them."

"Yeah, but I remember Basil Constant, that Brit from the Gnocchi case. Constant was supposed to be a famous postmodernist novelist, whatever the hell postmodernism is, but I found him to be a big creep.''

"You're much too critical, Talcott," said Hunter. "You don't have anything good to say about anyone, and everyone's a big creep. You probably think I'm a big creep, too. But you're afraid to say so."

Hunter looked at Weems and smiled.

"You? Not you! You know how to walk fairly well," said Weems. "Now I'll go and get that British professor. We'll see what light he has to shed on things."

Many of our experiences with electronic media are coded and stored in the same way they are perceived. Since they do not undergo a symbolic transformation, the original experience is more directly available to us when it is recalled. Also, since the experience is not stored in a symbolic form, it cannot be retrieved by symbolic cues. It must be evoked by a stimulus that is coded the same way as the stored information is coded.

The critical task is to design our package of stimuli so that it resonates with information already stored within an individual and thereby induces the desired learning or behavioral effect. Resonance takes place when the stimuli put into our communication evoke *meaning* in a listener or viewer.

—Tony Schwartz, *The Responsive Chord,* pp. 24–25

X EFFECTS

A SENDER
TRANSMITS
A MESSAGE
To A RECEIVER
THROUGH A
MEDIUM
WITH
X EFFECTS

Negel Hadley-Lassiter

"Tell me, Professor Haddley-Lassiter," Hunter asked, "what you recall . . ."

"Tell me, Professor Haddley-Lassiter," Hunter asked, "what you recall about the events of the past hour. What happened before the lights went out? Did you notice anything strange? Did anything happen to catch your eye?"

"Why, no," Haddley-Lassiter said, in a slightly nasal, high-pitched voice. "Nothing at all, Inspector. Of course, you must realize that I was thinking about my presentation and wasn't paying much attention to what was going on."

"What were you going to talk about?" asked Hunter.

"I've achieved a modest bit of attention," said Haddley-Lassiter, "for my work on communication theory. At one time, a number of years ago, what was called the hypodermic theory of media was popular. That is, we mass communication scholars thought that all members of an audience got the identical message from some television program or film or whatever. Then, thirty years later, we went to the opposite extreme, and some German professors argued, in a theory known as reader response theory, or sometimes reception theory, that nobody in an audience got the same message, since each person played a role in giving a text, which is what we call a television program or film or any work of popular culture or elite culture, its meaning. Or helping create its meaning. This idea gave readers and viewers a more important role in the creative process.

"We've had many other theories about the mass media," Haddley-Lassiter continued. Some have argued that they set agendas for people—that is, they don't tell people what to think but what to think about. The media focus our attention on certain things and ignore other topics; there's also the matter of how they present the topics they cover. Others have argued that they help shape our behavior because we wish to avoid cognitive dissonance, so we tune out messages that go counter to our basic beliefs. This would suggest that the most important aspect of mass communications is that they reinforce previously held beliefs.

"What I've done is more or less bypass these theories and look at the process of communication in some detail. I've suggested, in a very well known model, what communications scholars should consider when they do research. A model can be thought of as a way of diagramming or representing various relationships in something. My model can be reduced to a sentence, or perhaps formula would be a better term, that goes as follows: 'A sender transmits a message to a receiver through a medium with X effects.' "

"I don't understand," said Weems. "Why is that sentence such a big deal? I'm not an academic, so you'll have to explain it to me."

"Very simple," said Haddley-Lassiter, smiling. "My model, or that sentence, as you put it, points out the most important areas of concern for communication scholars. You have a sender, whom we can call A. He sends a message, which we will call B. He sends this message to someone, a receiver, whom we can call C. C can be a person or, in mass communication terms, an entire audience. The sender, A, uses a medium, which we will call D. And the message he sends has X effects. The X here stands for what happens as the result of the message being sent and received.

"For example, earlier Inspector Hunter said something to the effect of 'Weems, get two rooms for us to conduct our interviews.' The inspector is the sender, A. His message, B, was 'get two rooms for our inter-views.' You, Sergeant Weems, were the C, the receiver. The medium, D, he used was his voice. And the effect, X, was that you called the manager and obtained the rooms. But we can also use my model with the mass media and large audiences."

"And that's it?" asked Weems, with a puzzled look on his face. "Is that what happens in our universities nowadays? You think up a clever sentence and you get to lecture in conferences and universities all over the world?"

"Not quite," answered Haddley-Lassiter. "That sentence is the basis of a book I wrote, *The Process of Communication: Who Says What to Whom in Which Channel with X Effects*, that deals with each area in considerable detail. It's 450 pages long, with hundreds of footnotes. So you can see that there's a great deal to talk about when you deal with the communication process and that my formula is just the tip of the iceberg, so to speak. Mass communication theory is actually quite complicated."

"What good is it? What's it used for?" asked Weems. "I've read articles about research that's been done on specific things, like violence in the media, and I can understand what that might be important. But who gives a damn about any theory of communication, except, perhaps, a few professors like yourself?"

Haddley-Lassiter looked at Weems. "Another really stupid bobby," he thought.

"You've got to understand, sergeant, that everything we do in mass communication research is based on some theory or other . . . about how communication works, who it affects, how it should be studied. It's the same in all areas—whether it's science or the humanities or the arts. Theory is the driving force behind everything we do, and, if I may be so bold to state it, theory is basic and everything else is secondary. All the experimentation that goes on is based on proving or disproving some theory or something connected to some theory. In physics, for example, there are Einstein's theories that have shaped the experiments of physicists for many years. Think how important his formula $E = mc^2$ was. And the same could be said about medicine, as well. Practice without theory is blind. It's theory that tells you where to look and what to look for, what you should do research on."

"Just like in this case," said Hunter. "Professor, since you're an expert on theories, I'd be interested if you have any theories about who might have murdered Jean-Georg Simmul. Any ideas?"

Scratching his head, Haddley-Lassiter paused for a moment.

"This isn't my area of expertise, Inspector. I'm a professor of politics and media studies who writes material of interest to people in one small area of the academic world. I can tell you that Simmul was very controversial—to put it mildly. There are many scholars who consider him to be little more than a clever charlatan. His style of writing, one that is paradoxical and frequently unintelligible and opaque, had enabled him to pull the wool, as we say, over the eyes of scholars and intellectuals, not only in France but in America and many other countries. Other scholars, I must admit, think he's the most brilliant sociologist to come along in decades.

"A great deal depends on your orientation. Scholars in America tend to focus on what it called administrative research, which deals with making communication more effective and efficient. Their methods tend to be empirical. English and European scholars, as a rule, are more philosophical. They tend to come from what is called the critical tradition and are concerned about ideological matters such as the role of the media and society and how communication relates to social justice."

"I see," said Hunter. "So tell me, who do you think did it? Are you willing to make an educated guess?"

"You have to understand my background," replied Haddley-Lassiter. "I come from a rather conventional social science background, one that's empirical, so I regard people like Simmul as entertainers, as some kind of curious combination of scholar and comedian. He's very clever and very astute and wonderfully amusing and entertaining as a lecturer. Your question involves more personal matters, such as who in the room hated him enough to kill him."

"Did you know him well? What kind of a person was he?" asked Hunter.

"Actually, I don't think anyone knew him very well. He was very sociable, but you never felt you really knew him. He had, I've heard, a terrible temper, and he couldn't give up a grievance. So there were lots of people in the scholarly world whom he detested and quite a few people who couldn't stand him. Or even hated him. He could be, you know, quite nasty when he put that comedic public persona of his away."

"What was his claim to fame?" asked Weems. "Each of you who were on the panel must have some reason for being there. We know why you were there. Why was he?"

"He wrote a series of books on everyday life and different aspects of communication, in a style that is both highly suggestive and also incredibly ambiguous. So many people who wouldn't have agreed with him, if they understood what he really meant, thought they agreed with him. And he did have a wonderful style of lecturing. He talked about trivial things and read into them all kinds of symbolic and cultural significance. You could say he tried to read the universe in a grain of sand. His method could best be described a sociological semiotics—he was able to read objects and various kinds of behaviors as signs of other, more important things. The big question was whether he was reading what was there or reading his own ideas and prejudices into everything he dealt with.

"Was he a serious scholar who advanced hypotheses and then ran experiments to test them? Not at all. You could swear he made everything up as he went along. At least I and a goodly number of other scholars think that's what he did. Much of his material seemed like it came right off the top of his head, as if he'd say anything in an attempt to see what he could get away with. He was reputed to be a spy, you know. It was said he's been a member of the Deuxième Bureau for many years now. Maybe his being a spy contributed to his scholarly recklessness. He was very careful about some parts of his life and very careless about others—namely his ideas."

"I take it, from what you say, that you weren't good friends," said Hunter. "You certainly weren't on the same wavelength."

"As a matter of fact," said Haddley-Lassiter, "I rather liked Jean-Georg. We didn't see each other very often, but frequently when I was in Paris we got together for lunch. He knew, of course, all the best restaurants. When we got together, we would argue, for hours, about communication theory and politics. You don't have to agree with someone to like him—or her."

"Hmm," said Hunter. "What about the other people on the panel. Do you know anything about how they got along with Professor Simmul? I'm looking for some kind of a motive. Someone stuck a knife in his back, and there must have been a reason, a justification, at least in the killer's mind, for doing so."

"I really can't help you very much there. I was, as you know, farthest away from Jean-Georg when the lights went out."

"What were the other members of the panel doing? Did you notice?" asked Hunter.

"Before the panel began, I saw Elijah Ashdod-Sfard, the Israeli, chatting with Mikhaila, who was sitting between us. That would be perfectly natural."

"She's the knockout from Russia, not the old one, right?" said Weems.

"Yes, she is a knockout, as you put it. She's very beautiful and very smart and also very determined. I've always thought it best not to get in her way. She's left a legion of broken-hearted men, and any number of ex-husbands, in her wake."

"You one of them?" asked Hunter.

Haddley-Lassiter turned red. "Wha—what? You think I would fall for a woman like that? I find her attractive but rather common. I've a lovely wife who has infinitely more style and sophistication than Mikhaila. She's really, when you get down to it, just an overeducated peasant. When you question her, you'll see what I mean. Russia produces people like her in great numbers. They have no past, no class, no culture—just an astute mind and a keen intelligence. We were chatting a bit, as you might expect, while we were waiting for the panel to begin. She was giving me a recipe for borsht."

"What?" asked Weems. "Is that what you lofty thinkers talk about? She doesn't look like the domestic type to me. Not at all."

"I like to cook a bit," said Haddley-Lassiter. "And I told her I liked the food I had in Odessa when I lectured there last year. So she said, 'If you want to make good borsht, you have to cook some beef chuck, diced cabbage, and cut-up beets in a large pot, until they are soft.

Then you add some sugar, salt, and something called sour salt, which gives the borsht its rich flavor.' I intend to make some when I return home. My wife often is away lecturing, so I do some cooking. I find it relieves the tedium of it all. It's relaxing, if you don't have to do it all the time.

"Mikhaila, you should realize, is a seductress," added Haddley-Lassiter. "She has a fondness, it seems, for generals and high-ranking politicians, so I understand. I would interpret her behavior in Freudian terms, while she, no doubt, sees her behavior in Marxist and feminist terms."

"How does your formula explain a seductress like her?" asked Hunter.

"It's quite simple," replied Haddley-Lassiter. "Think about the way she dresses, her body language, the way she walks, her facial expressions, as well as what she says. All of these are messages that she sends, so to speak, to the person she intends to seduce. And what my formula calls the effect of her various messages is a seduction.

"The seductress, Freudians argue, is essentially id dominated, but she also uses her ego functions, which involve how an individual relates to her environment, because seductresses have to convince those they seduce to sleep with them—or indulge in whatever other form of sexual behavior they desire. The seductresses do this by using what Freud called our defense mechanisms, such as rationalization and suppression, to obtain the satisfactions they desire.

"It is possible to make a distinction between a woman who, at one point in time, becomes overwhelmed by desire and seduces a man and predatory seductresses like Mikhaila, who make a habit of seducing men. In the latter case we have behavior that Freudians might describe as an example of repetition compulsion, the need to repeat earlier experiences and certain behaviors as a means of obtaining sexual gratification and warding off unconscious anxieties and fears."

"It's amazing to me," said Weems, "the way you professors can explain everything."

"There are other ways of looking at the seductress, Sergeant Weems. From a Marxist perspective, which is her view on things, the seductress is a product of bourgeois beliefs and values and, in theory, is found only in capitalist economies. In socialist societies, where the sexes are, in theory at least, treated equal, sexuality is not an instrument of repression of the masses. Thus, there is no need for women to seduce men to obtain sexual gratification or anything else. Capitalist societies treat sexuality the way they treat everything else—as a commodity to be held in scarcity so it can be sold at a high price.

"In a sense, then, Marxists argue that the seductress in bourgeois societies is, without necessarily recognizing what she is doing, fighting against class domination and the control of the proletariat by the ruling class. The attitudes toward sex found in bourgeois societies are, after all, the ideas of the ruling classes—which use sexuality as a means of distracting members of the proletariat from class consciousness.

"Sexual behavior, Marxists argue, is ideologically conditioned. This means that seductresses are actually warriors on behalf the of the downtrodden and poor, who function to attack and help destroy the ideological chains that bind the proletariat and prevent it from obtaining class consciousness. Seductresses, then, Marxists argue, must be seen as waging war on the ruling classes; their behavior should be seen as part of the class conflict that ultimately will lead to the ruin of the bourgeoisie."

Haddley-Lassiter laughed.

"It's this kind of nonsense that Mikhaila believes, since it justifies her loose and predatory behavior. I can assure you, gentlemen, I never saw Mikhaila as a warrior for the proletariat. She's a woman who rationalizes her behavior with Marxist nonsense. Marxism is passé—it's dead! I used to be one, you know. Until I got religion."

"What about that Sfard character?" asked Weems. "What's his claim to fame?"

"Ashdod-Sfard?" said Haddley-Lassiter. "He's a typical Israeli. Imaginative, intelligent, and very arrogant. The Israelis actually think their universities are the best in the world. Quite ridiculous. He's famous for his work on what's called the silence spiral, which argues, in essence, that people who may be in the majority but think they are in the minority tend to be intimidated and silenced by people who think they are in the majority but are actually in the minority. He seems to find a way to attend every communications conference—at least the ones in the better cities."

"Tell me about the elderly German professor," said Hunter. "What can you tell us about her?"

"Lisa? She's been around forever, it seems. She's very frail now, but still manages to travel all over the world, popularizing her theories about the way audiences respond to the media, especially to what are called media events—things like the Olympics and royal weddings in England—events that billions of people watch all over the world. I don't think much of her work, but that's not important. I happened to overhear her telling Elijah that she wasn't feeling well and needed to get some medicine. So she left the room for a while before the panel began. And then she returned five or ten minutes later. She seemed to be terribly bored by Simmul's talk. I noticed she was glancing at her watch from time to time.

"That's one of the problems of being on a panel. You're trapped. If you're in the audience and you find a presentation boring, you can always slip out of the room. But if you're on a panel, you're stuck in place. Of course, sometimes, maybe even frequently, people on panels disagree with one another. Many panels are designed to let professors make their case and fight it out with other professors, who hold different views. They're the most interesting ones."

"Was this panel like that?" asked Weems. "From what you say, nobody on this panel agreed with anyone else about very much. Can't you professors agree on anything?"

Haddley-Lassiter laughed.

"But that's what scholarly life is like, Sergeant. We spend our lives trying to prove that we're right about something and those who disagree with us are wrong. We do it with our lectures, our articles, our research, and our books. What makes things complicated is that when you're dealing with people and communication, it's impossible to prove very much beyond a reasonable doubt. So there's lots of room for argument."

"That German woman, Professor Gurke—she was the person closest to Simmul. Think she could have stuck that knife in his back?" asked Hunter.

"That strikes me as utterly preposterous," said Haddley-Lassiter. "She's an elderly, frail woman. Lisa's actually a very sweet woman, when you get to know her. She's a bit shy, that's her problem. Besides, what reason would she have to kill him? It doesn't make sense."

"Maybe not," said Hunter. "That's what we've got to find out. The conference is going on for another few days and we probably will want to ask you some more questions, so please don't leave town without notifying us."

"Certainly," said Haddley-Lassiter. "I'm giving a paper the last day of the conference so I'll be around until then, for sure."

"Good. And thank you for your cooperation," added Hunter.

As he got up to go, Haddley-Lassiter looked at Hunter in an effort to get a sense of what he might be thinking, but he was utterly expressionless, so Haddley-Lassiter couldn't determine how well his interrogation had gone.

"He certainly is an enigma," Haddley-Lassiter thought. "He doesn't give anything away. I wonder how smart he is? Hard to know."

"Am I free to leave now?" he asked.

"Yes, but until I've interviewed all of the members of the panel, I'll have to ask you to remain in the suite with your colleagues," Hunter replied. "We might want to bring you back for more questions in a short while."

Hunter motioned to the policeman who was operating the tape recorder.

"Please escort professor Haddley-Lassiter back to the suite and bring Professor Vološinova here."

The policeman and Haddley-Lassiter left the room.

"What do you think?" asked Weems. "Could Haddley-Lassiter have done it? He'd have had time, since the room was dark for four or five minutes, so I understand."

"Hard to know, Talcott. When we've talked with the other members of the panel, we'll have a better idea of what the situation is and who might have been motivated to kill Simmul. I don't know what went on between the different members of the panel in the past. Were any of them lovers? Did any of them do something to make any of the others hate him or her? We've got to find out more about these professors. That will probably tell us something useful—maybe even something important. Right now, I don't have the slightest idea who might have done it."

What is the world according to television like? To discover its main features and functions, we have to look at familiar structures in an unfamiliar light. Rituals rationalize and serve a social order. They make the necessary and inevitable appear natural and right. In conventional entertainment stories, plots perform that rationalizing function. They provide novelty, diversion, and distraction from the constant reiteration of the functions performed by casting, power, and fate. The main points to observe, therefore, are who is who (number and characterization of different social types in the cast); who risks and gets what (power to allocate resources including personal integrity, freedom of action, and safety); and who comes to what end (fate, or outcomes inherent in the structure that relates social types to a calculus of power, risks and relative success or failure).

—George Gerbner, "Liberal Education in the Information Age," *Current Issues in Higher Education*

5

Mikhaila Blotnik-Kiev Vološinova looked scared.

Mikhaila Blotnik-Kiev Vološinova looked scared. Her eyes were red and hair was disheveled. She was a mess.

"This has been such a terrible shock to me," she said weakly. "I really liked Jean-Georg. He was a very delightful man, and incredibly modest, considering his accomplishments. What a tragedy."

She took out a small handkerchief and dabbed her eyes, for she had started crying again.

"Forgive me, please, for being so emotional," she said. "But I've never had an experience like this. I've never seen anyone I know murdered before."

"You can take a few minutes to compose yourself, Professor," said Hunter. "We understand how you feel. Can I offer you a cup of coffee? The manager has sent us up some coffee."

"No, thank you," she said. "I'm not in the mood to have anything."

After a couple of minutes, Mikhaila dabbed her eyes again and put her handkerchief away.

"Thank you, Inspector," she said. "You are most understanding. Now, how can I help you?"

"Please tell us something about yourself," Hunter said. "Tell us about your life, your education, your work."

43

"I'm afraid I've made a terrible mess of my personal life," she said. "You should know that I've been married and divorced four times. I keep making the same mistake, over and over again, it seems. I find a man who seems absolutely perfect, and we have a passionate courtship but inevitably, alas, a short marriage. After I get married to someone, I start discovering all the terrible flaws and shortcomings in him that I never noticed before. Maybe I expect too much? Maybe I'm not the kind of person who should be married? But, on the other hand, I really like men. I just can't seem to find the right one!"

She paused for a moment.

"It's a terrible problem. As you can see, I'm not unattractive, but my looks have been a curse rather than a blessing. I don't think I'll get married again. There are other arrangements that are possible now, thank heavens, that are more suitable for me. Marriage is, perhaps, too bourgeois an institution for our current postmodern era? The statistics about successful marriages aren't very good, and I've certainly done my share on that front." She laughed.

"Does that tell you want you need to know?" she added.

"We're not trying to pry into your personal life," said Hunter, "but we're looking for information that will help us find who the murderer was. Right now we've no leads to go on, and we're hoping that you and the other members of the panel might be able to help us."

"Yes, yes, I understand," Mikhaila said. "You're only doing your job. I was educated at the University of Moscow in linguistics and got my Ph.D. in that subject at the University of Tartu, where I worked with a scholar named Yuri Lotman. He worked on the semiotics of culture, and I developed a theory that argued that all creative works create their own futures but also are tied to works in the past. In the same light, there is a dialogue, so to speak, going on at all times in communication between people. Artists build upon the past when they create their works in the same way that conversations between people are connected to both previous conversations and anticipated future conversations.

"The word in living conversation is directly, blatantly, oriented toward a future answer-word: it provokes an answer, anticipates it, and structures itself in the answer's direction. Forming itself in an atmosphere of the already spoken, the word is at the same time determined by that which has not yet been said but which is needed and in fact anticipated by the answering word. Such is the situation in any living dialogue. What a person says is connected to the past and to the future. And the same thing applies to works of art, to what we call texts. Texts are all related to one another in the same manner.

"It's like these interrogations you are having, Inspector. The questions you ask are tied to what has happened in the recent past—in this case, the murder of the unfortunate victim, Jean-Georg Simmul—and to answers you anticipate, to some degree, in the future. His murder is probably tied to something that happened in the distant past, as well. This may seem like common sense to you, but many scholars, including some on the panel, have neglected this dialogic element in communication."

"I can understand where you're coming from," said Weems. "Your theory strikes me as reasonable. What I don't understand is how someone like Haddley-Lassiter can palm off his famous sentence—or formula—to so many people."

Mikhaila laughed again.

"There's much more to his work than that famous model of his, Sergeant," she said. "It's like a formula that contains a great deal of information in it. No, don't assume Haddley-Lassiter is famous because he wrote one sentence. It's like thinking Einstein was famous because he wrote one formula—$E = mc^2$. There's a rumor about that Haddley-Lassiter's a closet gay, you know. Could that be of any significance? Maybe Simmul was going to 'out' him?"

"You never know what's significant until you start putting all the pieces together," said Hunter. "What do you know about the other members of the panel?"

"Our Israeli friend, Elijah Ashdod-Sfard, the moderator, has a reputation for being quite a lecher. I don't know whether he does anything, but he spends a lot of time looking at beautiful young women and talking with them. Now if some beautiful young woman were to be his assistant, who knows what might happen. On the other hand, he may be just one more relatively harmless dirty old man. I told him he was a dirty old man when we were chatting. He's supposed to be a member of Mossad, or so I hear.

"In any case, Lisa interrupted us to tell him she was going back to her room, since she was feeling ill. I think she wanted to take some medicine. She came back in five minutes or so. The panel hadn't started because people were still coming in the room. That often happens at academic conventions.

"You might be interesting in knowing that the old crone Lisa Gurke was, in her younger days, reputed to be very beautiful and really wild. She was for a while, so I hear, a spy, like Ashdod-Sfard."

"Both of them spies?" said Hunter, in a shocked tone. "How do you know that?"

"I can't recall who told me, but it's widely known. Everyone knows about Elijah. Lisa was supposed to have been very high up in the Stasi, the East German intelligence service. A colonel or something like that. I don't know what she might have done for them. Seduced other spies? Killed them? Nobody seems to know what she did. This was many years ago, of course. She's been an important mass communication scholar for many years, though I've always felt she's been overrated. She hasn't been very productive for the past ten or twenty years."

"It's kind of interesting that you told us about her being a spy, Professor, because someone, I can't recall who it was—maybe Professor Haddley-Lassiter—told us that Simmul was a spy," said Hunter. So it's possible we had three spies, or former spies, on the panel at the same time. Remarkable.

"How would Professor Haddley-Lassiter know that? It may be true that Jean-Georg was a spy," added Mikhaila, "but I'd find it hard to believe. He was old enough to have been in the French Resistance. Maybe that's why he was described as a spy. Simmul was, you know, a genius. I think everyone on the panel was jealous of him. And he wore his brilliance lightly. He was always making witticisms and didn't take the scholarly life seriously, either. The French can be like that, you know. That really angered all those scholars who take themselves very seriously. Simmul was world famous, always lecturing at Harvard and Yale, but didn't make anything of his fame. He was actually a very sweet man. A bit shy, actually. He was always more interested in fun and games—with ideas, that is—than puffing himself up like many academics.

"Like anyone else in other occupations, some academics aren't the nicest people in the world when you really get to know us. For example, a writer once wrote the following about Simmul: 'At first I thought he was an absurdist, but then I realized he was an absurdity.' That writer was Elijah Ashdod-Sfard. He doesn't think much of Simmul's work. Simmul never forgave him for that insult."

"Were you jealous of Simmul?" asked Weems.

"Not at all," replied Mikhaila. "I know my limitations. And, of course,

I was so busy with marrying and divorcing my four husbands that I didn't
have time to be jealous. If you aren't disciplined, your personal life can
eat up all your time. That's what happens to most scholars. When they
are young, they have some big idea, some great goal they want to
accomplish. Then there are numerous interruptions—they get involved
in love affairs, raising children, travel, playing tennis—you name it. And
when they look around, at age seventy, they find that their life has been
the interruptions and they haven't accomplished their goal. It takes iron
discipline to do great things. I, alas, am not terribly disciplined, though
I've had one good idea, about the strategic importance of dialogue in
culture, and have made the most of it.

"In my younger and more foolish days I was a doctrinaire Freudian. I
believed that everything people do is based on unconscious impera-
tives, on the forces of their ids or desires fighting against their super-
egos or conscience, and moderated by the ego, which strove to keep
them in balance. I also believed in the Oedipus complex, as well—that
young children want to monopolize the attention of their parent of the
opposite sex. What nonsense!

"There is a basic ideological motif to Freudianism. A human being's
fate, the whole content of his life and creative activity—of his art, if he is
an artist; of his scientific theories, if he is a scientist; of his political programs and measures, if he is a politician; and so on—are wholly and exclu-
sively determined by the vicissitudes of his sexual instinct. Everything else,
I believed, represents merely the overtones of the mighty and fundamental
melody of sex. A person's consciousness is shaped not by his historical
existence but by his biological being, the main facet of which is sexuality.

"Now, of course, I am older and wiser and find Freud fascinating but
too unidimensional and simplistic. And I have four failed marriages to
prove that contention—though, I suppose, you could argue, from my
life history, just the opposite, couldn't you? Hmmm." A look of confusion and self-doubt suddenly flashed across her face.

"Thanks for your assistance," said Hunter. "You've been most help-
ful, Professor Vološinova. If we think of any other questions, we'll send
someone to fetch you. I'll have an officer escort you back to the suite."

"My pleasure," said Mikhaila. "I want to do anything I can to help
catch the murderer. How horrible!"

She got up and left the room, leaving behind a faint trace of Obses-
sion perfume.

Whether we are considering ordinary conversation, a public speech, a letter, or a poem, we always find a *message* which proceeds from a *sender* to a *receiver*. These are the most obvious aspects of communication. But a successful communication depends on three other aspects of the event as well: the messages must be delivered through a *contact*, physical and/or psychological; it must be framed in a *code;* and it must refer to a *context*. In the area of context, we find what a message is about. But to get there we must understand the code in which the message is framed—as in the present case, my messages reach you through the medium of an academic/literary subcode of the English language. And even if we have the code, we understand nothing until we make contact with the utterance; in the present case, until you see the printed words on this page (or hear them read aloud) they do not exist as a message for you. The message itself, uniting sender and receiver, in the quintessentially human act of communication, is simply a verbal form, which depends on all the other elements of a speech event to convey its meaning. *The message is not the meaning.* Meaning lies at the end of the speech event, which gives the verbal formula its life and color.

—Robert Sholes, *Structuralism in Literature: An Introduction*, p. 24

6

Elijah Ashdod-Sfard gave a nervous smile.

Elijah Ashdod-Sfard gave a nervous smile. "How can I help you, Inspector?" he said. "I was sitting fairly close to Jean-Georg, but then the lights went out and I couldn't see anything."

"Yes," said Hunter. "I understand. Did you, perhaps, hear anything? Did you notice anyone brush by you then? We're looking for whatever information we can get."

"No, Inspector. Nothing of the sort. People in the audience were shouting nervously about the lights being off, and then, after three or four minutes, maybe longer, they went back on—as mysteriously as they had gone off. It was then that I turned to my right and saw Jean-Georg. I was shocked, like everyone else. He was, you know, an agent of the Deuxième Bureau. His killing might have had something to do with that? Someone in the audience phoned 911, and they switched the call to the police, and you appeared on the scene with your crew. That's all I remember."

"Tell us something about yourself, Professor," said Hunter. "You can go back as far as you want. Tell where you were born, where you were educated, where you teach. The more detail the better."

"Yes," said Ashdod-Sfard. "I can understand. You are going to investigate everyone on the panel. It would be foolish to try and mislead you, and I have no intention of doing so. I was born in Russia, in Odessa.

49

When I was very young my family—that is, my mother and my father and myself—we moved to Israel and settled in Netanya. I was educated there, and then I went to the Hebrew University for my undergraduate work and my graduate work. I got my Ph.D. there in sociology. I secured a position at the University of Tel Aviv, and I've taught there all my life. I've had numerous visiting professorships at American universities over the years. You have to understand, the pay at American universities is very good. Our schedule at Tel Aviv allows this, fortunately."

"I see," said Hunter. "If you were trained as a sociologist, how come you're connected with these mass communication scholars?"

"It's probably something of an oversimplification, Inspector Hunter, but it's fair to say—or at least some people have argued that there really isn't a field called communication. Scholars from different fields study various aspects of it. There's only been a Ph.D. in communication in recent years, and most of the professors in the traditional disciplines are highly suspect about the communication Ph.D. What happens is that professors from the traditional social science disciplines, such as psychology and sociology, become interested in some topic that is tied to the mass media and so do some work in what is loosely called mass communication or the mass media.

"I became interested in the way that opinion is shaped in groups. My theory about the silence spiral refers to the fact that people who believe that their views are held by a minority tend to keep quiet while those who think they represent the views of the majority of people tend to make their views very well known. They boost their self-confidence and feel free to express their ideas, which they believe the majority holds.

"Those who think they hold the minority view, on the other hand, tend to keep silent so you get a cycle of silence on the part of those who think they hold the minority view. In fact, they may actually hold the majority view and not realize it. So this majority becomes silenced by a vocal minority that thinks it holds the majority view.

"You can see that this is, in essence, a sociological problem we're dealing with, since it involves groups of people and not the thought processes of individuals. The people who think they belong to the minority tend to overestimate the popularity of the views held by those who think they are in the majority and underestimate the strength of people holding what they thought were their minority views. People don't wish to be isolated from others, and this explains why some people keep quiet and others continually make their views known."

"Fascinating," said Hunter. "What your theory suggests is that people often don't know whether their opinions are shared by others. But what about opinion polls?"

"Actually," said Ashdod-Sfard, "you can't always trust opinion polls. People lie when they take them. And people who believe they are in the minority often refuse to tell pollsters their true beliefs. So frequently opinion polls don't help us find out what people really believe or what they intend to do—in an election, for example. The mass media have a major role in creating public opinion; they provide a kind of environmental pressure to which people respond with alacrity or with acquiescence—or with silence. Remember, individuals don't want to isolate themselves from others, and that becomes more important for them than their own judgment."

"Do you mean to tell me that all those opinion polls we read about in the newspapers are incorrect?" asked Weems.

Ashdod-Sfard smiled, and his bright blue eyes lit up.

"Not really," he said, "but you have to take them with a grain of salt. We know that people often don't tell the truth when you ask their opinion, so that has to be factored in. And sometimes the poll is biased in terms of the way questions are asked. It's quite complicated.

"What we media theorists do, as scholars, is investigate the role that mass media play in our lives and in our societies. And because people are so complicated, it is very difficult to be sure what impact the media have. For example, years ago mass communication scholars thought the media were very powerful. Then a decade or so ago they concluded that the media were relatively weak. Now the pendulum is swinging back, and most scholars are beginning to argue, once again, that the media are powerful.

"Then we have different approaches from different disciplines to further complicate matters. For example, anthropologists tend to look at the media in terms of myths and rituals that are tied to the content of the media and the way people use the media. Some theorists argue we use the media as a kind of play, an agent of pleasure and entertainment rather than persuasion. Others, in turn, say the media serve as gatekeepers, and though they don't tell us what to think, they do determine what we think about. We have many mass communication theorists who focus on the function of the media, in helping stabilize or destabilize society. I could go on and on."

"You already have," snapped Weems, who had an exasperated look on his face.

"Don't mind Sergeant Weems," said Hunter. "He doesn't have much patience and isn't interested in complicated matters. I appreciate your telling us all this. The picture I get of the scholarly world is that it is rather chaotic, with scholars disputing one another about almost every-thing—or, at least, many things."

"Yes," said Ashdod-Sfard, "but think how exciting that is. It's like warfare, except with articles and books and research instead of guns."

"I take it that since you were raised in Israel that you were in the army," said Hunter.

"Yes, of course," said Ashdod-Sfard. "Everyone, except for the very religious, serves in the IDF—the Israeli Defense Forces. Israel is a small country surrounded by many enemies. So everyone's in the army."

"What outfit were you in?" asked Hunter.

"Most of the time I was in the public information office, due to my background as a communication scholar. But I also was involved in combat, like almost everyone else in Israel."

"Hmmm," said Hunter. "Let me take a different tack. Did you know the victim very well?"

"I've been around so long that it's fair to say that I know all the important communication theorists tolerably well, though I must con-fess I never had much to do with Jean-Georg. We've been on many pan-els together and have lectured at a number of conferences, where we bumped into one another and chatted. I knew him, but not well, not like a friend. We haven't seen much of one another in years, actually. I have to confess that I don't like his work. I can't understand it, can't figure out how he gets his ideas and how he justifies them. I've been rather critical of his work—maybe I've been a bit too hard on him."

"What about the others on the panel?" asked Hunter. "We're you close to any of the others?"

"Not really. Not close. I, of course, know many of them. Same kind of relationship I had with Jean-Georg. I'm quite fond of Mikhaila, the Russian scholar. I call her 'the princess.' She's very beautiful, but it hasn't led to a happy life, poor thing. I know Lisa quite well. And I've been on an occasional panel with Nigel Haddley-Lassiter, but I don't know him well at all."

After saying Haddley-Lassiter's name, a look of hatred, perhaps revulsion, flashed across Ashdod-Sfard's face for an instant. Hunter did not miss this, however, and filed it away in his memory.

"Do you get along with all of them?" asked Hunter. "Have you had any personal relationships with any of them? Any fights about methods? Any fights about anything? Anything of interest you can report?"

"No, sorry, I can't tell you that much about them. We bump into one another from time to time, over the years. But it's more of less like my relationship with Mikhaila. We are at conferences together, we might have dinner together from time to time, but we each go our own way after we give our lectures or whatever."

"So you have no opinion—dare I use that word to you—about who, on the panel, might have wanted to kill Professor Simmul?"

"None at all," said Ashdod-Sfard. "It was a terrible shock to me— and to everyone on the panel, too. I'm sure of that. It must have been someone who came in the room when it was dark and killed him. But why? I don't have the slightest idea. Simmul was actually a very pleasant man, and he had many friends—and no personal enemies that I can think of, though I should be fair and indicate that there are many scholars who disagree with him about this or that—and maybe everything? He was controversial, you know."

"Did you know there was a rumor that Professor Simmul was a spy?" asked Hunter.

"I find the idea rather preposterous. You don't find professors who are spies—as a rule, that is. Our lives, generally speaking, are not that exciting."

"Could Haddley-Lassiter be the killer?" asked Hunter. He wanted to see how Ashdod-Sfard reacted.

"Haddley-Lassiter?" said Ashdod-Sfard, with a tone of incredulity. "I would seriously doubt that. He's one of those English twits, you know. Boarding school at an early age, Eton, Oxford—the whole British upper-class received pronunciation bit. He's very bright but a bit of a jerk. I can't imagine him killing Simmul—or anyone, for that matter."

"If there's nothing else you can think of to tell us, we'll let you return to the suite where your colleagues are waiting," said Hunter. "Thank you so much for all the information you shared with us."

Ashdod-Sfard got up to leave.

"We'll send an officer to escort you to the suite," Hunter added, "and then we'll interview the last member of the panel, Professor Gurke."

"I wouldn't take everything she tells you as the gospel," said Ashdod-Sfard, as he left the room. "She's getting old, and her imagination sometimes gets the better of her. Lovely woman, though."

Evidence in support of the claim that the media have sizable direct impact on the public is weak as regards each of the dozen most often-mentioned intended or unintended effects of the media. The most commonly mentioned intended effects include: (1) the influence of commercial advertising on buying behavior; (2) the impact of mass media political campaigns on voting; (3) public service announcements' efficacy in promoting beneficial behavior; (4) the role of prolonged multimedia campaigns in changing lifestyles; (5) monolithic indoctrination effects on ideology; and (6) the effects of mass-mediated ritual displays on maintaining social control. The most often cited unintended effects of the mass media include: (1) the impact of program violence on viewers' antisocial aggression; (2) representation on the media as a determinant of social visibility; (3) biased presentation of media as a influencing the public's stereotyping of groups; (4) effects of erotic materials on objectionable sexual behavior; (5) modes of media presentation as affecting cognitive styles; and (6) the impact of introducing new media on public thought processes.

—William McGuire, "Who's Afraid of the Big Bad Media?" in *Media USA,* 2d ed., p. 274

7

"How can I help you?" asked Lisa Schauber Gurke . . .

"How can I help you?" asked Lisa Schauber Gurke, as she walked into the room in a slow and unsteady manner. "You'll forgive me," she said, "but between my age and my illnesses, and the shock of Jean-Georg's murder, I'm not feeling very well. Not well at all." She sat down slowly, then took a small handkerchief with her left hand and dabbed some perspiration from her brow. She was a short woman, perhaps in her late sixties, with curly gray hair and light green eyes.

"You seem to have taken his murder very hard," said Weems. "I can understand. There's always something traumatic about seeing a person with a knife sticking out of his back."

At this, she shuddered. There was a look of terrible sadness on her face.

"I was sitting right next to the man," she replied. "We had been chatting about various things. We're old friends, and we were . . . were . . . once very good friends. Then the lights went out, and when they went back on, poor Jean-Georg—he had that horrible knife in his back. So you see, Sergeant Weems, I have good reason to be upset."

"Yes, of course," said Hunter, trying to soothe her nerves. "You can

take a few minutes to relax and compose yourself, and then we'll continue with our questions."

"I'll be all right," she said. "I'll be happy to answer any questions you
might have . . . and help in any way I can."

"Would you like a cup of coffee?" asked Hunter. "It might calm your
nerves."

"No, thanks," she replied. "If I have coffee, I'll be even worse than I
am now, but you're most kind to ask."

"Please tell us something about your background," said Hunter.
"We're trying to find out as much as we can about each of the members
of the panel to see whether that information leads anywhere. Right now
we have nothing to go on."

"I was born in 1932 in Düsseldorf and grew up there. After I graduated from our version of what you would call high school, I attended the
University of Berlin and got my Ph.D. in psychology in 1972, at the age
of forty. I then taught in a small provincial university for a year, until I
got my chair at the University of East Berlin, where I've been since 1973.
I've been a visiting professor, sometimes for a semester and sometimes
for a year, at a number of universities, such as Harvard, New York University, Oxford University, the University of Paris—places like that."

"You get around a great deal, don't you?" commented Weems.

"You might say that," said Gurke, with a faint smile on her face.

"Were you ever married?" asked Hunter. "Did all those visiting positions interrupt your life, or did you like being away from Berlin at those
universities?"

"No," said Gurke, somewhat sadly, "I never married. I once thought
I'd be getting married to someone, but . . . it didn't work out."

"Sorry to hear that," said Weems.

"Yes," replied Gurke. "However, one can live quite nicely as a single
person. Not everyone needs to be married, and to tell you the truth, I
don't know whether I'd have been happy if I got married. I'm a rather
independent sort of person, if you know what I mean. I have a compan-
ion with whom I've been living for a number of years."

During this conversation between Weems and the professor, Hunter
was watching her carefully. She seemed to be a rather fragile, elderly
woman, but something about her, about the way she held herself, about
the way she talked, bothered Hunter.

"Tell us something about your work in mass communication theory. We've been getting quite an education from the professors we've been interviewing," said Hunter.

"When you talk to professors, you always further your education," she replied. "After all, that's what we're paid for. In any case, I've done a good deal of work, in recent years, on what could be described as televised worldwide media events—occurrences such as royal marriages, Sadat's visit to Israel, the Olympics—that is, what might be called televised ceremonial events that have an international character and are of interest to people all over the world. I wanted to find out why people watched these events, what they expected to get from them, how they reacted to them, how they were influenced by them. When you have hundreds of millions of people doing anything, I've always believed it demands some kind of a scholarly investigation. And that is what I've done my research on—televised public events.

"Television provides its events with a narration, with a scenography and with a scenario. It displays in each case an inventiveness, which explains why so often spectators with direct access to the event would rather opt for watching it on their screens. A public event has a table of contents that we spectators must memorize, and it relies on a cultural repertoire with which we must become acquainted. Narrators offer spectators an introduction to its program, a description of its itinerary, a rehearsal of its highlights, a profile of its participants. Once it really starts, the event repeats an already-known pattern, fulfills a temporal expectation, unravels a melody that the viewers could already sing for themselves. . . ."

She paused for a moment to collect her thoughts.

"These events are very complicated and quite a challenge, I must say. Before I became interested in media events, I did research on how audiences use the media. I investigated the uses people make of media and the gratifications the media provide to people. If you knew anything about the field of mass communication research, you would know that I'm a bit of a contrarian. Most of the research at the time focused on the effects of media on people. I took the opposite tack and looked at how people made use of the media. You could say that my work on media events is a kind of follow-up to my research on uses and gratifications. This field of research, I should add, is not popular nowadays.

Younger scholars tend to be more ideological and interested in feminism, postmodernism, and nonsense like that. At least I think it's nonsense."

"I see," said Hunter. "I've never come across this notion of uses and
gratifications before. Could you tells us a bit more about these uses and
gratifications, perhaps give us some examples?"

"Of course," she said, straightening up in her chair. "Let's take the
medium of television, for example. My theory is that we should consider
how viewers of particular television programs make use of these programs. We can say that in general people want to be entertained and
amused. They want to see villains in action, because villains are often
more interesting than heroes, but they also want to see heroes triumph
and reinforce the notion that good triumphs over evil.

"They often like to see authority figures made fun of and deflated,
though sometimes they like to see them exalted. Viewers of television
like to satisfy their curiosity about things and learn about what's going
on in the world, and they want to connect with what is exalted and
beautiful in the world, and sometimes to identify with the deity and
things of that nature. Some viewers are looking for models to imitate
and people with whom they can empathize. Others are searching for
ways to experience, in a guilt-free and controlled manner, extreme and
powerful emotions—such as love and hate, horror and terror. Some
want to be purged of unpleasant emotions by watching television, and
others want to participate, vicariously, in history.

"Let me take a particular genre or kind of program to show all this.
Let's take science fiction shows like *Star Trek*. There are heroes like Kirk
and Spock, there are villains galore—different kinds of aliens and mon-
sters—and there is generally some kind of battle that the heroes win.
Viewers get to see the various villains in action and can participate
vicariously in their villainy, knowing that ultimately the villains will not
succeed. The program may satisfy their curiosity about outer space and
provide them with information they didn't know. I think you can see that
there are a number of uses viewers of *Star Trek* can make of the program
and gratifications they can get from it. And the same, of course, applies
to every program."

"I see," said Hunter. "It sounds very reasonable to me."

"Yes," said Lisa Schauber Gurke, "but this theory has been attacked as too impressionistic and not yielding empirical data. It's hard to generate statistics when you do uses and gratifications research, and some critics argue that researchers can read anything they want to in the texts they analyze. That is, a given act in a television story can be interpreted many different ways, as providing any number of different gratifications. Most contemporary media researches are intoxicated by numbers."

She smiled.

"How tedious this argument becomes. I happen to think that empirical studies, full of data, are only mildly interesting and not as scientific as the empiricists believe. Because after you have your data you have to interpret it, and different scholars, from different schools of thought, can interpret the same data in different ways. So we're all open to criticism. We spend our lives defending our methodologies and attacking our opponent's methodologies. I'm afraid there's no royal road to perfect research, though a lot of younger scholars seem to think there is."

"I don't get it," said Weems. "Why the hell can't all you media researchers agree on anything? What goes on in universities? I get the feeling we're paying big bucks to a bunch of prima donnas who have a hell of a good time going to conferences all over the world, often at taxpayers' expense, to argue with one another—when they're not eating at our best restaurants, that is. To my mind, you find some research subject that interests you, you find the facts, and you report what you found. What's so complicated about that?"

A faint smile came to the professor's lips.

"I'm afraid it isn't that simple, Sergeant," she said. "We can measure how many hours women spend watching soap operas, for example, and we can interview these women and ask them why they like soap operas. We can get their answers and try to figure out what their answers reveal. But human beings are very complicated, and we can never really know why anyone does anything. People lie to others, they lie to themselves, and they give researchers answers they think they want to hear.

"We can never know, for sure, why people do anything. And we all do the best we can to answer this question of why, recognizing that our answers must always be considered incomplete. For example, something happens. We can generally find out what happened, when it happened, how it came about, where it took place, and who was involved. We can't always be sure about how accurate our information is, but it is possible to be fairly well satisfied about what our research has uncovered. But why it happened—that's the problem."

"Speaking of why questions," said Hunter, "do you have any idea why someone might want to murder Professor Simmul?"

"That's beyond me," she said. "I had come back from my room, where I went to get some medicine. I'm not well. I suffer from asthma, among other things. Shortly after Jean-Georg gave his presentation, the lights went out and there was a great deal of confusion in the room. People were shouting. Then the lights went on. It was horrible. I'll never forget that nightmarish scene."

"You've never seen a murdered body before, I take it," said Hunter.

"Why, no, of course not. I'm a professor at a university, and I've led a sheltered life, as you would say," she answered. "I really liked Jean-Georg. At one time I . . . I . . . loved him. We had an affair many years ago. I assume you'll find this out when you proceed with your investigation. But we drifted apart. You know how things like that happen."

"What happened?" asked Hunter.

"It's hard to say. It's always little things, trivial things, that start adding up, and before you know it a relationship is dead. It's very hard to maintain a relationship, very hard. But we've remained good friends."

"I see," said Hunter. He looked at the professor, who now was remarkably composed. "If you've nothing more to tell us, you may go back to the suite where the others are waiting. If you do think of something, I urge you to get in touch with us immediately. We'll have an officer escort you back to the suite where the others are waiting."

"Yes, I most certainly will," she replied. She got up and slowly left the room with halting steps.

"What do you think?" asked Weems, after she had left the room. "She comes across as a fragile old lady, but somehow, for some reason, I feel it's just an act."

"I agree with you," said Hunter. "We'll get the dope on her and all the others later on, when we get the reports from their universities and from Interpol and find out what our intelligence people have been able to dig up on these professors. She was the closest one to Simmul, so it would have been easiest for her to stick that knife in his back. And it doesn't take that much strength, either. I've got my doubts about her, too."

"I guess it's a kind of intuition," said Weems. "I wonder if the communication professors study that?"

"Maybe we ought to think about this murder in terms of her uses and gratifications theory. What gratifications could the killer get from sticking a knife in Simmul's back? In what way might killing him be useful? And to whom? Something to think about. Now, let's take a look at Simmul's room. Then we'll go down to the suite where the professors are waiting for us. Have someone tell them that we'll be letting them go in just a short while."

"Will do," said Weems, as he took out his cell phone and started tapping on the key pad.

There is a basic principle that distinguishes a hot medium like radio from a cool one like the telephone, or a hot medium like the movie from a cool one like TV. A hot medium is one that extends one single sense in "high definition." High definition is the state of being well filled with data. A photograph is visually "high definition." A cartoon is "low definition," simply because very little visual information is provided. Telephone is a cool medium, or one of low definition, because the ear is given a meager amount of information. And speech is a cool medium of low definition, because so little is given and so much has to be filled in by the listener. On the other hand, hot media do not leave so much to be filled in or completed by the audience. Hot media are, therefore, low in participation, and cool media are high in participation or completion by the audience. Naturally, therefore, a hot medium like radio has very different effects on the user from a cool medium like the telephone.

—Marshall McLuhan, *Understanding Media: The Extensions of Man,* pp. 22–23

8

"Simmul's room is surprisingly neat," . . .

"Simmul's room is surprisingly neat," said Weems, as he and Hunter opened the door and walked inside. "I thought it would be a mess. You know how these eggheads can be incredible slobs. They're used to having other people look after them all the time, tell them how wonderful they are, take care of their every need."

"He's spent some time resting in his bed," said Hunter. "But he's done a tolerable job of making it up again, as if, maybe, he were expecting a visitor? His shoes are lined up and his books and papers are in neat piles. Probably because he's a writer. They tend to be very disciplined and organized."

"Yeah," said Weems, looking over the things that Simmul had left on his desk. "Here are a couple of his books: A *Critique of the Significance of the Sign*—probably more of that semiotics nonsense. Here's another one, *New Perspectives on the Consumer Society*. I'll be it's another one of those high-brow attacks on advertising and societies where people buy lots of things. If people don't buy things, other people don't make them—and sell them. I just wonder what he had in his house in Paris, or wherever he lived. I doubt that he lived like a monk."

"Let's give the room a good look," said Hunter. "There may be something in here of interest that will point us toward his killer. Let's do it systematically, too. We'll look at everything, including the undersides of all the drawers, the toilet—everything."

"OK," said Weems. He opened a dresser drawer and started looking through it. "Just some shirts and that kind of stuff," he said. He started pulling out the drawers, one by one. "Nothing interesting so far."

"Make sure you look in the space under the bottom drawer. People sometimes stash stuff there," he said.

Hunter had gone to Simmul's bag—a large leather one with a relatively narrow base and high sides. He opened it and starting examining the contents.

"Nothing much so far," said Hunter. "The usual stuff—shirts, pajamas, underwear. He was a professor, and there's no reason to assume we'll find anything other than what you generally find in hotel rooms—clothes, dirty underwear, toothbrushes, and that kind of stuff. But you never know what you'll find."

"Yes, I agree," said Weems. "He was murdered, and it certainly is worth a bit of time looking around."

"We'll keep sniffing about, like good hunting dogs. You never can tell what we'll come up with," said Hunter. He was looking at Simmul's suitcase. He pulled out a book.

"Here's a murder mystery," said Hunter. "It's by a Japanese writer, Hideo Nagoya. Ever hear of him?"

"No," Weems answered. "I only like American and British mystery writers. I don't like the ones foreigners write; I can never follow them. They're too esoteric, generally speaking."

"This one's called *In a Garden*."

"Funny name for a murder mystery," said Weems.

"You know the Japanese," replied Hunter. "They do things differently than we do. And they have this love of gardens that's quite remarkable. They spend enormous amounts of money on them, so I understand." He opened the book to page one.

Softly fell the blossoms from the cherry trees. They drifted down to the ground, carried by a gentle wind, in lazy spirals. Inspector Yukio Hottokikki Daidokoro of the Central Tokyo Police Department sat silently in a secluded spot in the Kiyosumi Gardens, lost in thought. There was a grisly murder that had taken place and he had few clues. Birds were singing sweetly and the sun filtered through the trees. A white male of about fifty had been found shot to death in Shinjuko, at the top story of the Sumitomo building. His fingertips had been cut off, so it was impossible to use fingerprints to identify him. There were no identification papers on him. The labels on his clothes had been ripped out. All his hair had been shaved from his body. But in his teeth a small fragment of tempura was discovered, and his stomach also revealed that he had eaten a tempura dinner approximately three hours before he was murdered. "Hmm," thought the inspector. "Tempura is stripped of the meaning people in the West attach to fried food, which is heaviness. Here in Japan flour recovers its essence as scattered flower, diluted so lightly that it forms a milk and not a paste; taken up by the oil, this golden milk is so fragile that it covers the piece of food imperfectly, reveals here a pink of shrimp, there a green of pepper, a brown of eggplant, thus depriving the fry of what constitutes the Western fritter, which is its sheath, its envelope, its density. This tempura, so Japanese, yet actually Portuguese, is the only clue we have. . . .

Hunter put the book down. "Very strange, even from the little I read to you, Talcott—you can see that. Pretty gruesome, too. But then, those Japanese gangsters are supposed to be maniacs."

"Slow moving and boring, full of ridiculous asides. That's why I stick with good American mystery writers like Mickey Spillane and Paul Auster," said Weems. "I like writers who know how to tell a good story, without going off on tangents or having detectives spend time with idle speculations on trivial matters."

"Funny, but there isn't that much room in this suitcase," said Hunter, who had resumed examining its contents. "Could it have a false bottom?" He picked it up and looked at it and then started probing around. "I'll be damned," he said. "There's a false bottom to this thing. Who would have thought it?"

"Sometimes they sell bags like that for people to hide money and valuables," said Weems.

Hunter took out a small penknife and started prying at the bottom part of the suitcase. He slipped off a detachable piece of the suitcase's false bottom and found a small area in which there was a thin parcel.

"I've found something," he said, taking out a small flat parcel that was lightly wrapped. "Looks like this package was opened before. What could this be? Think he was on drugs?"

Hunter pulled the wrapping material off the parcel.

"I think we might have found something important," he said. "There are two little packages in this one." He opened the first. He looked at a thin piece of white plastic, which he smelled. In the next he found some small detonating caps.

"This is incredible," said Hunter. "Simmul was carrying a plastic bomb and some detonating caps. What the hell is that kind of stuff doing in a professor's suitcase?"

"Bombs?" said Weems. "But why?"

"I don't have the slightest idea. But it seems that the good professor was up to more than analyzing postmodern culture or whatever it is he did. We've got to get the dope on him from Interpol and our other sources. He could have been working for the Deuxième Bureau or he could have been a mad bomber, on the loose. God only knows what he was up to—and what he did before he was killed!"

"Think it could be spy stuff? If so, we ought to get in touch with the FBI," said Weems.

"Let's see what else we can find, if anything, before we get them involved in this case. He may not have been involved in espionage at all," said Hunter.

"Just a simple ordinary professor who had one curious habit—he liked to carry plastic bomb-making equipment with him," added Weems.

"It's Sentex, the Czech stuff," said Hunter, looking at it carefully. "Where in blazes did he get this? Let's finish searching this room and then beat it to headquarters and see what our researchers in intelligence have been able to find about this group of professors. Now that I think of it, didn't Ashdod-Sfard tell us that Simmul was a spy? How did he know?"

"I thought Ashdod-Sfard said it was preposterous to think that professors might be spies," Weems replied.

"Well done, Weems," said Hunter. "It was Haddley-Lassiter who told us about Simmul. Glad to see you're paying attention. Ashdod-Sfard seems to have a rather exalted view of the importance of professors—at least of professors like himself."

"Yes," replied Hunter. "But a lot of the professors involved in our cases had very high opinions of themselves. It seems to be an occupational disease."

"On the other hand," continued Weems, "it seems that everyone who we interrogated other than Ashdod-Sfard told us that one or another of the professors on that panel is a spy. I don't think we can rely on anything any of them tell us. They mix up truths, half-truths, and lies. All of these professors know a lot more than they're telling. That seems to be pretty evident. They only tell us what they want us to know. That's the problem of dealing with very intelligent and devious people.

"I'm sure glad I didn't become a professor, Hunter. It seems to be a rather cutthroat business, from what I can tell. I'd rather deal with out-and-out criminals—with them, at least, you know what you're getting. You can't believe anything they tell you, and that makes life a lot simpler."

"I think you're being too harsh on professors," said Hunter. "Remember, we've only dealt with a rather unusual sampling of professors—those involved in murder cases. Most professors are ordinary citizens, who lead rather conventional lives. They teach their courses, grade their papers, complain about their students and the administration, and try to find ways to advance their careers. Just like anyone else. Now let's see what Dominick Wimmer in our intelligence section has found."

But when does one isolate oneself? The individual tries to find this out by means of a "quasi-statistical organ": by observing his social environment, by assessing the distribution of opinions for and against his ideas, but above all, by evaluating the strength (commitment), the urgency, and chances of success of certain proposals and viewpoints.

This is particularly important in changeable circumstances in which the individual is witness to a struggle between conflicting positions and has to consider where he stands. He may find himself on one of two sides. He may discover that he agrees with the prevailing (or winning) view, which boosts his self-confidence and enables him to express himself with an untroubled mind and without any danger of isolation, in conversation, by cutting those who hold different views. Or he may find that the views he holds are losing ground; the more this appears to be so, the more uncertain he will become of himself, and the less he will be inclined to express his opinion. . . . Thus the tendency of the one to speak up and the other to be silent starts off a spiraling process which increasingly establishes one opinion as the prevailing one.

—Elizabeth Noelle-Neumann,
"The Spiral of Silence: A Theory of Public Opinion,"
Journal of Communication, p. 44

"We've been really busy," said Dominick Wimmer . . .

"We've been really busy," said Dominick Wimmer, head of the intelligence section research team at the police headquarters. He greeted Hunter and Weems when they arrived at the police headquarters the next morning. "We've got a lot of information that I've put together for you. Hope it helps."

"Thanks," said Hunter. "This is a tough case, and the more we know about our international cast of academic all-stars, the better."

Wimmer gave Hunter a manila folder with papers in it. "Here's all the stuff we got about the professors," he said. "They all came in as e-mail, and these are the print-outs. I've summarized them all and sent you the information as an e-mail message. You can read my summaries on your computer screens or in the hard copy here."

"Thanks," said Hunter. He took the folders and walked to his office, which he shared with Weems.

"I'm dying to find the scoop on these professors," said Weems. "It sounds crazy, but from what we've heard, at least two of them were spies. Maybe three?"

"Why not?" asked Hunter. "Professors don't make that much money, as a rule. They've plenty of time on their hands, and they get around a lot. It's a good cover, especially since everyone thinks professors are more or less harmless, with their heads in the clouds about their areas of research and scholarship. We, of course, know better."

"That's a good point," said Weems.

A few minutes later they were sitting at Hunter's desk. He had turned on his computer and called up his e-mail.

"Let's start with Simmul," said Hunter. He pressed a couple of keys on his keyboard, and the screen with the information about Simmul popped up.

JEAN-GEORGE SIMMUL

French. Professor of Social Semiotics, University of Paris X. 1968 to present. Born in Lyons in 1929 to the former Berthe Poularde and Yves Simmul, a horsemeat butcher. Attended the University of Lyons from 1948 to 1952. Then went to the University of Paris. Doctorate awarded in 1960. Dissertation: "The System of Consumer Culture." Taught at Lycée Jean-Matilde Benoist, 1960 to 1967. Professorship at University of Paris X starting in 1968. Married to Juliette Barthes in 1950. Known to be a member of the Deuxième Bureau from 1970. Cellule Bleu.

"What's Cellule Bleu?" asked Weems.

"The Deuxième Bureau is the French spy system," Hunter replied.

"Cellule Blue is a special unit connected with finding moles and double agents. The important thing is that we know, now, that Simmul was a French spy. So whoever killed him could have done so in connection with his being in the Deuxième Bureau or for some other reason, not connected with it all. Simmul may have been after a mole or double agent, which is why he had that plastic bomb-making material."

"I wonder what he did with it?" said Weems.

"I'm afraid somebody's going to find out," replied Hunter. "And they won't find it a pleasant surprise, at all. Let's see what they've found out about Dr. Gurke."

LISA SCHAUBER GURKE

Professor of communication at the University of East Berlin, since 1973. Born in Nuremberg in 1932 to Ilse Schtupp and Franz Gurke, a podiatrist. Educated at the University of Düsseldorf for B.A. and Ph.D. in psychology in 1972. Dissertation subject: "Uses and Gratifications by Housewives of Network Television in Düsseldorf, 1963–1965." Author of three books on communication. Single. Known to be member of Stasi since 1973. Currently living with Mimosa Rakutani, Japanese science fiction writer.

"I'll be damned," said Weems. "Another spy. It just blows my mind. I wonder whether Gurke killed Simmul? She was sitting next to him, after all. And maybe she was sent to San Francisco to get rid of him?"

"Probably," said Hunter. "But it may have been something personal, too. She did say that she had a relationship with him, after all. She may have been nursing a grievance for a number of years and suddenly snapped. He wouldn't be the first person killed by a woman who resented the fact that she'd been dumped by him."

"Who's next?" said Weems.

"Let's look at Ashdod-Sfard. He was sitting next to Gurke, between her and Vološinova."

ELIJAH ASHDOD-SFARD

Born in Odessa, Russia. Moved when a child with family to Netanya, Palestine (now Israel), in 1928. Educated in primary grades at local kibbutz and then, from junior high school on, at Yeshiva Sarton-yam Ben Yehuda. Attended the Hebrew University in Jerusalem from 1948 to 1952 and later University of Tel Aviv from 1952 to 1958, obtaining doctorate in 1958. Subject: sociology. Dissertation topic: "Political Socialization in Kibbutz Kelev, 1950–1955." Married to Natalie Pagum, 1950. Divorce, 1955. Marriage to sociologist at the University of Tel Aviv, Shoshana Manishevitz, in 1960. Colonel, Israeli Defense Forces, Air Force. Reputed to be member of Mossad from 1955 to present.

"Let's move on to Vološinova," said Hunter, clicking a couple of keys. The description of Vološinova came up on the computer.

MIKHAILA BLOTNIK-KIEV

Born in Pinsk in 1966 to Svetlana Marozhenoye and Simeon Tzaddik Vološinova, a minor bureaucrat in the Pinsk sewer department who moved to Minsk when Mikhaila was a young child. Educated in private schools in Minsk and began university education in 1985 at the University of Moscow. Marriage in 1987 to Dimtri Vechnoyepero, opera singer. Marriage annulled three months later. Marriage to Yvgeny Klyever, banker and sportsman, in 1989. Divorce in 1990. Marriage to Spencer Margolis, English journalist in 1991. Divorce in 1992. Marriage to Sven Stikkelsaber, Norwegian diplomat in 1992. Divorce in 1994. Ph.D. in linguistics in 1994, University of Tartu. Subject: "Bakhtin's Theory of Dialogism." Thought to have been recruited into OGPU in 1996.

"OGPU! Another spy!" blurted out Weems. "It's just too much. I'm beginning to think every one of these characters was a spy. She really got around, didn't she? She is beautiful, but with a track record like that, you'd think any guy who got involved with her would be a bit scared."

"With good reason," said Hunter. "She hasn't been married for a while now. Maybe she's decided it's not worth the bother. Nowadays, you don't have to be married to have a good sex life."

"I'll bet she does," said Weems. "Still, I don't know whether the guys who get to go to bed with her should consider themselves lucky or should be pitied. She's a scary dame."

"Not scary," corrected Hunter. "Demanding!"

"That's what I mean," answered Weems. "Demanding women are scary. I give up. As far as I'm concerned, they're all spies. I wonder whether the professors in some of those other cases we were involved with were spies. They could have been; we never pursued that angle."

"Look, Talcott," said Hunter. "Just because the professors we've investigated so far have all been spies doesn't mean that Haddley-Lassiter is a spy or that all professors are spies. Even if Haddley-Lassiter is a spy, it doesn't mean that we have to jump to the conclusion that many, or most, professors are spies. There may be something going on at this meeting, which we don't know anything about yet, that drew all these people here."

"I'll bet Haddley-Lassiter is a spy," said Weems. "There are too many spies for it to be a coincidence, Hunter. I'll bet this organization is a front for some international spy agency and that all these communications professors are spies."

"We'll soon find out. Haddley-Lassiter is next," said Hunter. The description of Haddley-Lassiter popped up on the screen.

IGEL SIMON HADDLEY-LASSITER

Son of Emma Smith-Lumpen and Basil Edward Horace Clive Haddley-Lassiter, stockbroker and horseman. Born in 1962 in London. Attended Eton and then Oxford, where he took a first in political sociology in 1988. Ph.D. dissertation topic: "Power Relationships: A Study of Fashion Advertising in *The Times*, 1965–1970." Appointed reader in politics at Sussex University in 1988; in 1992, senior reader; in 1996, professor of politics and media studies at the London School of Economics. Marriage in 1990 to Margery Seawell, psychiatrist and playwright.

"Nothing about Haddley-Lassiter being a spy," said Hunter. "It looks like at least one of these professors on the panel isn't a spy?"

"Maybe, but it wouldn't surprise me to find out that Haddley-Lassiter really is a spy, just that we don't know about it," replied Weems. "I mean, how come you have a panel with five professors on it, and the first four of them turn out also to be spies?"

"You may be right, Talcott, but for the moment I'm going to work under the assumption that he isn't a spy. I want to keep everything as simple as I can," said Hunter. "Here's the coroner's report. Wonder what he found?" He started reading.

"Here's something," he said. "Simmul was stabbed by a left-handed person. The coroners have a way of knowing this, based on how the knife blade entered the body and where it ended up. That's very interesting."

"Why?" said Weems.

"Did you notice, Talcott, when Professor Gurke dabbed her eyes with her handkerchief, when we interviewed her earlier, she did it with her left hand? She's left-handed. Now the pieces of this puzzle are beginning to fall into place. Let's go and talk with Professor Gurke again. I've got some more questions I want to ask her. The professors are all at the Hilton, attending the conference. Let's get over there and see what she has to say."

"I'll get a car and driver, and we'll go back to the Hilton. It should only take ten or fifteen minutes."

"Good," said Hunter. "And let's take a couple of officers with us. Who knows? We might need them."

In the dictionary the mass is defined as the great body of the people of a nation, as contrasted to some special body like a particular social class. Lazarsfeld and Kendall use such a definition when they write "The term 'mass' then, is truly applicable to the medium of radio, for it more than the other media, reaches all groups of the population uniformly." This notion of the mass merely implies that a mass communication may be distinguished from other kinds of communication by the fact that it is addressed to a large cross-section of a population rather than only one or a few individuals or a special part of the population. It also makes the implicit assumption of some technical means of transmitting the communication in order that the communication may reach at the same time all the people forming the cross-section of the population.

—Eliot Friedson, "Communication Research and the Concept of the Mass," *American Sociological Review*, p. 313

AT A CRUCIAL POINT, INSPECTOR HUNTER SPECULATES ON MURDER

"Nobody's seen Professor Gurke since last night," . . . .

"Nobody's seen Professor Gurke since last night," said Weems. "She was supposed to give a presentation at a session this morning, but she didn't show up."

"Who was the last person to see her?" asked Hunter.

"I already checked into that," said Weems. "The clerk at the key desk spoke with her. She came in around 10:30 PM, picked up her key, and went up to her room. She told the clerk she'd been to Masa's and had one of the best meals of her life. He said she seemed a bit unsteady on her feet; he thought it might have been a bit too much wine."

"Masa's? People don't usually go there by themselves. Have someone get in touch with Masa's and find out whether she was with anyone and if so, what they looked like. Meanwhile, let's get someone to let us in her room. She's been ill and may have had some kind of attack. She may need help. Or something might have happened to her."

They got a clerk to take them to her room, on the twentieth floor of the Hilton. He opened the door.

"If you need anything else, let us know," said the clerk, who turned and went back to the lobby.

"Thanks," said Hunter.

When they entered the room, they saw her lying in her bed. Hunter rushed over to her and felt her pulse.

"She's dead," said Hunter. "It looks like she died shortly after she got back from the restaurant. We'd better get the team here to check out the place. I wouldn't be surprised if she's been poisoned. Have the coroner check her over. And let's see if we can find out what she did after I released everyone from that suite last night.

"I'll be damned," said Weems. "I was sure she was the person who killed Simmul. Now it looks like I was wrong."

"Not necessarily," said Hunter. "I'm pretty sure she killed Simmul. But there are some questions I need to answer. The first is, why did she kill him? The second is, who killed her? And why? This case is getting really complicated now. Her death may be connected with all this spy business. It looks like we've got a den of spies here, and these murders might be tied to that. But we can't know for sure. It might not be that at all."

Weems took out his cell phone and punched in some numbers. He had a brief conversation and hung up.

"I've taken care of everything. The team will be here to dust for fingerprints and see whether they can find anything. The coroner will give the professor's body a thorough examination. And we've sent someone over to Masa's to find out whether the professor was dining alone."

"Good," said Hunter. "Now, let's look around her room. We might find something interesting."

"Maybe another bomb kit," said Weems. "I wouldn't be surprised at anything that happened in this case."

Hunter walked over to a small table near the window. On it there were copies of some of the papers that had been given at sessions she attended, several books, and a stamped and sealed letter.

"This might be worth looking at," said Hunter. "It's addressed to a professor in England, Damien Worley, at Goldsmith's College in London, so she probably wrote it in English. A bit of luck on our part."

Hunter took out his penknife and slit the envelope open. He took out several pieces of paper on which the letter had been written and started reading it.

"Anything exciting?" asked Weems.

"I think you'll find this letter most interesting," said Hunter.

July 14, 2000

Dear Damien:

I've been meaning to write and respond to your last letter. I just got into San Francisco for the Global Communication Association meetings that start in a couple of days. I always like to arrive early so I can catch my breath, so to speak. As you know, I've not been feeling well lately. I move slowly now, like a turtle, but if I give myself enough time, I find that I can somehow manage to get where I want to go and do what I want to do.

Thank you so much for your kind invitation to give a lecture at the Conference on Media and Culture that you've organized. It will be good to see you and your colleagues again. I happen to be free in April, and, assuming my health holds up, I will be most happy to attend, especially since I really adore London. It is, as I've told you many times, my favorite city. I love the way the men dress in the city, and I adore going to all the wonderful shows that you always find in London's theater district. There's also a great deal of superb music in London, and the quality of the restaurants has improved greatly, so I hear.

I'm writing this from the Hilton Hotel in San Francisco. The people who live in San Francisco believe that they are living in the center of the universe. It is a beautiful city, but it is also terribly provincial and in many ways uninteresting. I still love the European cities, which are beautiful and which also have character.

San Francisco does have a good symphony and a decent opera and ballet, but there's relatively little good theater here, and the newspapers are third-rate. There are some excellent restaurants. Considering that only 700,000 people live here, that San Francisco is actually a rather small city, I guess the residents here have something to be proud about. They also are fortunate to be near the University of California at Berkeley and Stanford, two outstanding educational institutions, as good as anything we have in Europe. And maybe better? Don't tell your friends at Cambridge and Oxford I said that!

Parts of the city are quite handsome, but, curiously, nearby there are some very shabby sections and the streets are full of homeless and various other lost souls—religious fanatics, bums, alcoholics. It can be quite depressing to walk in the downtown area. If you go south of the Hilton, you find yourself in a kind of skid row.

I've been thinking about what I might deal with at your conference. I was thinking of doing something on the television show Survivor *that was so popular in America in recent months. I had a former student tape all of the episodes for me and want to do an analysis of the program. My thesis is that* Survivor *was really a combination of many different popular genres, so different people liked it for different reasons. For example, the women tended to wear rather scanty clothes a good deal of the time. They were often in bikinis. So it had elements of the* Baywatch *beach bunnies kinds of programs, with voluptuous women in scanty bathing suits running around a beach.*

At the same time, the various people in the show—Rich, Greg, Colleen, Stacey, Kelly—they were all involved in intrigues and alliances, and you never knew who was double-crossing whom. There were, then, elements of the soap opera in the show, with its many complications and intrigues and tangles.

There were also sport show elements in Survivor. *Many of those immunity challenges were like games or sports contests, created by those who created the show. So the players had to use various strategies to win these contests. Winning an immunity challenge was important because it guaranteed that you wouldn't be voted off the island—that you would survive for another week. The voting they did had a strong ritualistic element to it, which made you think you were watching some kind of anthropological documentary at times. The setting, the torch bearing, the clearing in the jungle—all were designed to suggest mythic rites.*

Could there be, I sometimes wonder, elements of the Adamic myth in this game? After all, Adam was thrown out of paradise, and the "players" in Survivor *who were voted out were "cast out" of this island paradise, though in many respects it seemed like the reverse of paradise. Of course, there was a big difference. Everyone playing the game in* Survivor *was in it for the money—for the million dollars that the last person on the island would win. When we were thrown out of the Garden of Eden, the price we paid was immortality. As I get older, I become more conscious of this—with every passing day, I must confess. My days, I recognize, are numbered; I just hope the number is a large one and doesn't come up too soon.*

I might also say something about the fact that the show was highly edited, so we didn't get reality but a simulation of reality that focused on personal relationships, intrigues, gossip, and that kind of thing. I think the editing was brilliant and the camera work was superb; it reminded me of the kind of profiling that happens in sports games, where the director and announcers start focusing on certain players and creating rivalries and generating drama. Viewers probably didn't think about all the quick cutting, all the vignettes, all the material about the lives of the characters, or when the people on the island talked directly into the camera, at the viewers. But that was very effective.

Survivor *isn't a reality program but a pseudoreality one. The idea was imported from Sweden, if I recall correctly. The success of this show now poses a challenge to traditional narrative shows like soap operas and situation comedies. The most significant shows in America this year have been* Who Wants to Be a Millionaire *and* Survivor. *It will be interesting to see what happens with the new season in America. I might deal with this a bit in my talk, also.*

So—how does that sound? One could probably argue that Survivor *was a drawn-out media event, which would suggest it is the kind of text, a new kind of media event, that I have dealt with in recent years in my research.*

In a couple of days I'll be giving several papers. One of them will involve being on a panel with Jean-Georg Simmul. I've always avoided him as much as I could since our relationship ended, so bitterly, years ago. But the fates have put me in the

*same room with him. Mikhaila Blotnik-Kiev Vološinova is also,
by chance, on that panel. She has not spoken to me for many
years—ever since she found out that I was the person who prevented her from getting that chair at Harvard. I felt it wasn't right
for her and hoped that they might give it to me. How she ever
found out about my role in that matter is beyond me. Perhaps
Jean-Georg told her? Very few people knew about it. In any case,
she wrote to me earlier and said she wants to put the past behind
us and make up. We are to have dinner at a very fine restaurant
that she knows about. It seems that one must make reservations
months in advance to get a place. So maybe this sad history of
enmity between Mikhaila and me will be put to rest. I believe
she may have got religion or something? She claims that she's a
changed woman.*

Warmest regards,
Lisa

"Wow," said Weems. "It looks like Mikhaila was the one who went
with her to dinner at Masa's."

"And poisoned her!" said Hunter. "It certainly is a possibility. It's
quite likely, now, that professor Gurke killed professor Simmul and that
professor Vološinova killed professor Gurke."

"God. I always thought being a professor was as safe and boring a
job as one could possibly imagine," replied Weems. "Now it looks like
we had a panel of five professors, and four of them were spies."

"And two of them, so it seems, were murderers," said Hunter. "I
thought we'd never see anything like that case in which Glioma, the
demented literature professor from Cal Berkeley, killed off the entire
board of editors of his journal, *Shakespeare Studies*, because he thought
they were going to take the journal away from him. This case strikes me
as almost as bizarre."

"I remember how each of them had an interpretation of *Hamlet* that
was different from all of the others. It was pretty wild," said Weems.

"Let's see what Dr. Mikhaila Blotnik-Kiev Vološinova has to say for
herself," said Hunter. He picked up the phone and dialed the operator.

"Please connect me to the room of Dr. Vološinova," he said. He waited while the phone rang. Nobody answered.

"She's not there! Damn!" exclaimed Hunter. "Who knows where she could be? Maybe we should try her room. God only knows what we might find."

The principal thesis of the sociology of knowledge is that there are modes of thought which cannot be adequately understood as long as their social origins are obscured. It is indeed true that only the individual is capable of thinking. There is no such metaphysical entity as a group mind which thinks over and above the heads of individuals, or whose ideas the individual merely reproduces. Nevertheless, it would be false to deduce from this that all the ideas and sentiments which motivate an individual have their origin in him alone, and can be adequately explained solely on the basis of his own life-experience. . . .

Only in a quite limited sense does the single individual create out of himself the mode of speech and of thought we attribute to him. He speaks the language of his group; he thinks in the manner in which his group thinks. He finds at his disposal only certain words and their meanings. These not only determine to a large extent the avenues of approach to the surrounding world, but they also show at the same time from which angle and in which context of activity objects have hitherto been perceptible and accessible to the group or the individual. . . . Strictly speaking it is incorrect to say that the single individual thinks. Rather it is more correct to insist that he participates in thinking further what other men have thought before him. He finds himself in an inherited situation with patterns of thought which are appropriate to this situation and attempts to elaborate further the inherited modes of response or to substitute others for them in order to deal more adequately with the new challenges which have arisen out of shifts and changes in his situation. Every individual is therefore in a two-fold sense predetermined by the fact of growing up in a society: on the one hand he finds a ready-made situation and on the other he finds in that situation preformed patterns of thought and conduct.

—Karl Mannheim, *Ideology and Utopia*, pp. 2, 3

11

MIKHAILA'S JOURNAL ENTRY

After the party I took a walk... and had a fantastic surprise. I am positive I saw Nyle Hobbley-lassiter wearing women's clothes. He was prancing around Market Street in a kinda weird a long skirt. I heard he was a bisexual but didn't know he was a transvestite... Too bad, because he's not bad looking.

"She's not in her room," said Weems . . . .

"She's not in her room," said Weems, as he walked into Vološinova's room. "At least we don't have another dead body on our hands."

"At least not here," said Hunter. "And maybe, I hope, not anywhere. But there is a pattern to all this that I'm beginning to see. The members of the panel seem to be killing one another in a kind of murder-go-round. The questions now are, where is she and what is she doing with herself? If she's still alive, that is. Put out an all-points alert for our people to find all of the professors who were on the panel and ask them to get in touch with me—immediately. I made a mistake in not having each of them tailed. Of course, I didn't have that information about them from Interpol and our others sources to guide me."

"It's hard finding people at conventions like this," said Weems. "If they're not on a panel, they could be anywhere. Lots of them come to these conferences to see their friends, and they're all over the place, having something to eat, going to the museums. It's tough, but I'll see what we can do."

He picked up his cell phone again and started punching numbers into it. While Weems was on the phone, Hunter looked around Professor

Vološinova's room. He picked up a few books stacked on a table. One was Denis McQuail's *Mass Communication Theory: An Introduction*. Another was a book called *Theories of Mass Communication* by Melvin L. DeFleur and Sandra Ball-Rokeach. She also had a book titled *Modern Criticism and Theory* edited by David Lodge, and something called *Rabelais and His World* by a Russian named Bakhtin.

"Doesn't seem like the most enjoyable kind of bedside reading," thought Hunter, "But these academics live in a world all of their own."

He picked up another book that was a hardback with a simple black cover. He opened it up. It was her journal.

"What a stroke of luck," he thought. "This might have something interesting in it." He started reading.

July 15, 2000. San Francisco.

I arrived here in the late afternoon and went to a party being thrown by one of my publishers, Oxford. Lots of the big names in mass communication scholarship were there, drinking champagne and gobbling up the hors d'oeuvres. You had to be assertive to get anything to eat. So I stationed myself in front of the buffet table and made sure I got some chicken wings and shrimp and a bit of salad. From looking at the list of speakers and their papers, it seems most of the people at the convention are from little-known schools in the middle of nowhere. And some of the bigger schools are in horrible places, like Michigan State and Iowa State and the University of Nebraska. What a horror, to be marooned in a desolate place like the middle of Minnesota. It's like being sent to Siberia. There are some speakers from first-rate schools, like New York University, the University of Chicago, and MIT, but most of them are from nonentity places with too many names— Southwestern Louisiana State University or Eastern Michigan State University. Glorified teachers colleges, I imagine. Maybe I'm too much of a snob? But if you're in Russia and not at the University of Moscow or Leningrad, let's face it, you're in the provinces. My years in Tartu were enough for me.

None of the men at the party, alas, looked particularly interesting or desirable. It's hard finding a good-looking man with a good head on his shoulders. I understand a large percentage of the men in San Francisco are gay, so that makes things very difficult for the poor women who live here. Of course many of them may be lesbians. So maybe it evens out and the heterosexual men and women find one another, somehow.

After the party I took a walk—and had a fantastic surprise. I am positive I saw Nigel Haddley-Lassiter wearing women's clothes. He was prancing around Market Street in a blonde wig and a long skirt. I'd heard he was a bisexual, but I didn't know he was a transvestite. Too bad, because he's actually not bad looking. Some English men are very handsome. Others have those long pointy noses and big elephant ears like poor Prince Charles. It was terrible how he and the royals treated that poor Diana. She was a breeding mare, when you get down to it. With our czars, you didn't have any problem getting rid of people. They poisoned one another or found some other way to get rid of competitors. Stalin used firing squads. There are many ways to rid oneself of people you don't want around or detest, for one reason or another.

During my walk I noticed that there a number of people speaking Russian with a Jewish accent. It looks like half of Odessa is here. There are also quite a few Russian restaurants in the city. Quite surprising. I was astounded by the number of people who are homeless. They wander the streets pushing metal shopping carts they steal from supermarkets that are loaded with blankets, clothes, and all kinds of junk.

I've got to do a bit of work on an article—a comparison political discourse in Russia, Ukraine, and Byelorussia. I'm sure the world is eagerly waiting to hear what I have to say. At least it is on a serious subject and is of theoretical interest, unlike most of the simple-minded papers listed in the program—on trivial matters like popular music and the comics. They take trivial subjects and use the most complicated and affected kind of language to talk about them. They probably learn it in graduate school. If I hear people talking about problematics, reification, reflexivity, and that kind of nonsense any more, I think I'll scream. I've other work to do here, too. I can't waste too much time at the sessions or going to parties.

At the Oxford party I met a strange little man, one Albert Fess, from some French university. He has a scraggly beard and was always fidgeting. He's a sociologist, one of those postmodernists who isn't interested in traditional sociological questions but studies things like shopping malls. I don't know why sociologists forget about the important theoretical problems—socialization, propaganda, power, opinion research, rumor, functional analysis, things like that.

It turns out that Fess has written a book titled Minotaur: The Beast in the Shopping Mall, *about something called the Mall of the United States in Minnesota or Kansas. I can't recall where. Maybe it was the Mall of America? Perhaps I'll buy a copy later to see what he has to say about these malls. He mentioned that a few years ago he was involved in planning an international conference on postmodernism that never materialized. The professor who was planning it, from the University of California at Berkeley, was murdered.*

Professors are, let's face it, human beings who have their disagreements and in some cases their hatreds, for any one of a number of possible reasons. Sometimes the reasons are valid. So it isn't as far-fetched as it might seem to have professors who are also killers! In America, it seems that every day there are hundreds of murders, many of which are never solved. The Americans seem to have a love affair with guns and don't want to give them up. The antigun politicians are powerless, it seems. In my Freudian days, I'd say these gun owners are suffering from a diffuse form of castration anxiety, but now I would search for other reasons.

I want to go to Macy's and Neiman-Marcus and some of the other stores that are very near here, and see if I can find some nice clothes. Clothes are so expensive in Russia and not very stylish, though this is changing a bit. There are lots of nice stores here in San Francisco, which is one of the reasons I like coming here.

Later this week I'm going to some restaurant named Masa's with Lisa. I told her that I've forgiven her for preventing me from getting that position at Harvard, and she believes me. Poor thing, she looks terrible. I think she may be failing. I made the reserva-

tions months ago; it is supposed to be the best restaurant in San Francisco and very expensive. I'm sure it will turn out to be a most memorable meal for Lisa.

Weems had made his call to put out an all-points bulletin for the remaining professors when his cell phone rang. Picking it up, he said, "Weems." He listened for a moment. "OK, I'll tell the inspector right away."

"What happened?" asked Hunter, putting the journal down.

"Haddley-Lassiter has committed suicide! He seems to have jumped out a window earlier this morning. He was taken to the morgue, and a few minutes ago somebody there was able to trace his fingerprints. He didn't have any identification papers on him. Funny thing. They're doing an autopsy. He was a mess—his head was all bashed in, too. Probably from the fall."

"I can't believe he killed himself," said Hunter. "It would be too much of a coincidence. It turns out now that three people from that panel have been killed. Two of the deaths were definitely murders. This one seems like a suicide, but it breaks the pattern. No, I'll bet that either the Israeli professor, Ashdod-Sfard, or Professor Vološoniva did it. I think we'll find that one of them killed him and dumped his body out a window. But why?"

"Haddley-Lassiter, as far as we know, wasn't a spy, either, " said Weems.

"These murders," said Hunter, "I'm beginning to think now, had nothing to do with espionage, killing moles and double agents, and that kind of thing. I think we had a panel of people who hated one another so violently, who nursed grudges so long that they began to fester and made each of these people irrational, so that the professors all have been involved in killing the person they hated most."

"So," said Weems, "what's our next step?"

"Let's go to Haddley-Lassiter's room and see what's there," replied Hunter. "With these professors, you never know what you'll find when you go to their rooms. Nothing would surprise me now, I must say."

The research and theory of gatekeeping had originated in the work of Kurt Lewin who, in 1947, studied processes of decision-making with regard to household food purchases. He observed that information always flows along certain channels which contain "gate areas," where decisions are made. This idea was taken up in 1950 by David Manning White. He studied the processing of information by telegraph wire editors in American newspapers, whose decisions to discard news items coming over the wire was seen as the most significant gatekeeping activity. In 1969, this theory was revisited by A. Z. Bass, who differentiated among different gatekeeping roles. He argued that the most important gatekeeping activity occurs within the news organization, involving two stages, news-gathering and news-processing.

—Chaim Eyal, personal correspondence

12

"Nothing here," said Weems . . .

"Nothing here," said Weems, when they opened the door to Haddley-Lassiter's room. "The bed hasn't been made. Guess the maid hasn't got around to his room yet."

"It is pretty early," Hunter said. "Maids generally wait until later to make up the beds. Let's take a look around and see what we can find. Take a look at his dresser. I'll see what's on his desk."

Hunter walked over to the small desk in Haddley-Lassiter's room and started examining the objects on it. He picked up a slim volume.

"Get this," said Hunter. "Here's a curious little book, *Postmortem for a Postmodernist*, that claims it teaches its readers about postmodernism and also entertains them by being a mystery story. It has quotes and a comic-strip frame before each chapter. Most unusual."

"That's the most ridiculous thing I've ever heard of," said Weems. "A mystery story should be about murder and criminals. If you have stuff on postmodernism or any other subject, you don't have a mystery—you have a weird kind of textbook. People who read mysteries want entertainment. They don't want some egghead trying to teach them some-

thing about some obscure and useless philosophical movement. Nowadays it seems editors will publish almost anything."

"I agree," said Hunter. "But remember when we were involved in the
Gnocchi case. From talking with all those professors, I got the notion
that in postmodernism, you can mix things up however you want to, so
maybe this book is a good example of postmodernism. Maybe postmodernism is anything you want it to be and postmodernists do whatever they want and use postmodernism to justify things. Do you remember the way one of the professors described it—'a blending of genres,
irony, stylistic eclecticism'? Maybe that's it? *Postmortem for a Postmodernist*
is a new, postmodern kind of textbook?"

"There doesn't seem to be anything here in the dresser," said
Weems, as he pulled out the drawers and looked in them. "Did you find
anything?"

"Here's something. Haddley-Lassiter was going to submit a proposal
for a new book to a publisher. Maybe it has something of interest?"

IN THEIR OWN WORDS: THE GREAT MASS COMMUNICATION
THEORISTS SPEAK FOR THEMSELVES

In Their Own Words is unlike most books on mass communication theory, in which writers take the ideas of the major theorists and paraphrase
them, water them down with an occasional quotation here and there, and
so on. In this book I will focus my attention on using quotations of no
more than 2,000 words by our most important mass communication
thinkers. I will supply some context and analyze these quotations, but the
major thrust of this book will be on the ideas of the most seminal mass
communication theorists in their own words. Thus, those who read this
book will be able to see exactly what these theorists wrote. My book also
will differ from edited readers, which reprint entire articles or long selec-
tions from theorists. I know, from experience, my students do not have
the patience to read long and difficult articles and that they get bored
reading traditional textbooks, which tend to be dull and simplistic. Let me
offer some examples of what I have in mind. You can think of this book
one that goes to the heart of the matter and leaves off material of secondary interest.

Example 1

Professional persuaders are often concerned with research on source, channel, and message variables . . . but audience variables have been given the most attention by students of mass communication. Why does the same message, delivered through the same channel, from the same source, succeed in affecting the attitudes of one person and not of another?

Four characteristics of audiences seem to be particularly important in accounting for different attitudinal effects. First, there are personality and educational differences; some people are more easily persuaded than others, some can understand more complicated arguments, and so on. Second, people are situated in a variety of social settings; one person's friends and family may be liberal, while another is in a more conservative milieu. Third, the attitudes that any one person has may vary in strength; he or she may be deeply committed to a given church or political party, may be more loosely attached, or may have no attitudes at all on some political and religious subjects. Fourth, external events may affect audience attitudes; a communication that is not very persuasive in peacetime may be quite compelling in time of war—or vice versa.

W. Phillips Davison, James Boylan, and Frederick T. C. Yu, *Mass Media: Systems and Effects* (New York: Praeger, 1976), 174.

Example 2

[F]rom our point of view, the media audience is not to be understood as mere consumers who passively accept anything that the media offer, but as active individuals and members of social groupings who consume media products in the context of their personal and social goals. In modern societies, that means quite a lot. Because the media system plays such an important role in society, linking the audience to all its various institutions, it is necessarily the case that the media will play important social and personal roles in individual and collective life.

Sandra J. Ball-Rokeach and Muriel Cantor, *Media, Audience and Social Structure* (Thousand Oaks, Calif.: Sage, 1986), 17, 18.

Example 3

If all good art has no rhetorical dimension, as so many have argued, then the "rhetoric" is left to those who will use it for the devil's purposes. . . . How much better it would be if we could develop a way of understanding how great literature and drama does in fact work rhetorically to build and strengthen communities. Reading *War and Peace* or seeing *King Lear* does change the mind, just as reading *Justine* or taking a daily dose of TV fare changes minds. A movie like *The Graduate* both depends on common-places shared much more widely than our slogans of fragmentation and alienation would allow for, and strengthens the sharing of those com-monplaces; like *The Midnight Cowboy* or *Easy Rider*, it can be said to make a public as well as finding one already made. All of them work very hard to appear nonrhetorical; there are no speeches by anyone defending the graduate's or the cowboy's values against the "adult" world that both movies reject so vigorously. But the selection from all possible worlds is such that only the most hard-bitten or critical-minded viewer under forty is likely to resist sympathy for the outcasts and total contempt for the hypocritical aging knaves and fools that surround them. If sheer quantity and strength of pressure on our lives is the measure, the rhetoric of such works, though less obvious, is more in need of study and the open aggres-sive rhetoric of groups like *The Living Theatre*.

Wayne Booth, "The Scope of Rhetoric Today" in *Rhetorical Dimensions in Media: A Critical Casebook*, ed. Martin J. Medhurst and Thomas W. Benson (Dubuqu, Iowa: Kendall/Hunt 1984), xvii.

Example 4

Let me describe how my theory of vicious cycles works:

1. As a result of childhood and other television viewing, children develop a fear of becoming and adult since that is seen as being involved in adult conflict.
2. This fear children develop, of being an adult, leads, in turn, to their incapacity to have and to sustain satisfactory emotional relationships.

3. Almost inevitably, this inability to have good relationships, in turn, leads to fear of marriage, fear of feeling, and non-relational sex.

4. These behaviors are unsatisfying to those involved, leading to pain, anxiety and various kinds of escapism, such as television viewing and drugs to obtain "relief."

5. Television viewing then becomes, for many people, an electronic narcotic upon which they become dependent, in an effort to escape from their sense of imprisonment within themselves—to have mediated, vicarious, parasocial "relationships" with others, and so on. But while television may provide relief, it also reinforces unconscious childhood fears. Thus it helps create the very dependencies that television viewers use it to escape from, making people, in a sense, "prisoners" of their television sets and, ultimately, prisoners of themselves.

Arthur Asa Berger, *Human Behavior* (Los Angeles: Manson-Western, 1984).

Example 5

Cultivation theory has been developed primarily by Gerbner and his associates. Its basic thesis is that the symbolic world of the media, particularly television, shapes and maintains—i.e. cultivates—audiences' conception of the real world (in other words, their construction of reality). Television, with its presence in the vast majority of American homes, is said to be the common symbolic environment into which most children are born and thus the most pervasive source of exposure to everyday symbolic cultures that Americans share or have in common. The symbolic world of television is shown by content analysis to be a "mean" world where violence is commonplace. Violence is used by most TV characters, usually to gain the upper hand in struggles for power. The young, white, males who dominate the TV world as leading characters also dominate others, particularly women, minorities, and old people, via the successful use of violence. According to cultivation theory, this violent white-male dominated TV world seeps into viewers' consciousness so that they see the real world as being like the TV world.

Melvin L. DeFleur and Sandra Ball-Rokeach, *Theories of Mass Communication,* 4th ed. (New York: Longman, 1982), p. 207.

Example 6

Simplifying to the extreme, I define *postmodern* as incredulity toward meta-narratives. This incredulity is undoubtedly a product of progress in the sciences: but that progress in turn presupposes it. To the obsolescence of the metanarrative apparatus of legitimation corresponds, most notably, the crisis of metaphysical philosophy and of the university institution which in the past relied on it. The narrative function is losing its functors, its great hero, its great dangers, its great voyages, its great goal.

Jean-François Lyotard, *The Postmodern Condition: A Report on Knowledge* (Minneapolis: University of Minnesota Press, 1984), xxiv.

I think you will find this book solves the problem of how to teach mass communication theory to students who have shortened attention spans, due to their immersion in television, and who may also have little or no interest in the subject. It is often the case that students take courses such as mass communication theories because they are required courses.

"To me," said Hunter, "he's proposing a glorified book of quotations. Seems like he was taking the easy way out."

"I think you're right," said Weems. "It's pretty evident that he doesn't have a very high opinion of students. I don't know what it is with these professors. They hardly do any work and nowadays many of them seem to hate their students almost as much as they hate the administrators of their institutions. I guess they'd prefer to have universities with no administrators and no students—just professors. They could do research, chat, and play tennis whenever they felt like it."

"We've wasted enough time on Haddley-Lassiter's proposal," said Hunter. "Let's get back to work. Take a look in the closet and in the bathroom."

"OK," said Weems, walking into the bathroom. "Nothing here."

Hunter opened the closet. Mikhaila Blotnik-Kiev Vološinova's body was stuffed in the closet. She had a small bullet hole in the middle of her forehead.

"Damn," said Hunter. "Haddley-Lassiter's killed Vološinova. He must have got her to come to his room, on some pretense, and then shot her. This means only Ashdod-Sfard's still alive—that is, if he is still alive. We've got to work fast now."

Weems had taken out his cell phone and started pecking at the numbers. After a few seconds, someone answered his call and he had a brief conversation.

"I'll have a squad over here right away, and I've asked one of our officers to come and guard this room. This case is beginning to get to me. The killings don't seem to stop. There's one murder after another."

"Let's see if we can get to Ashdod-Sfard in time," said Hunter. "He may be out of the loop and not involved in all this, but it looks to me, given what's happened so far, that he killed Haddley-Lassiter, after Haddley-Lassiter had killed Vološinova. She was a really beautiful woman. She'd said that she'd made a mess of her life, but she was still young enough to set it straight, if she had had the time. Too bad she never got the chance."

The text as such offers different "schematized views" through which the subject matter of the work can come to light, but the actual bringing to light is an action of *Konkretisation*. If this is so, then the literary work has two poles, which we might call the artistic, and the aesthetic: the artistic refers to the text created by the author, and the aesthetic to the realization accomplished by the reader. From this polarity it follows that the literary work cannot be completely identical with the text, or with the realization of the text, but in fact must lie halfway between the two. The work is more than the text, for the text only takes on life when it is realized and furthermore the realization is by no means independent of the individual disposition of the reader—though this in turn is acted upon by the different patterns of the text.

—Wolfgang Iser, "The Reading Process:
A Phenomenological Approach," in *Modern Criticism and Theory*, p. 212

Elijah Ashdod-Sfard's mind was racing.

Elijah Ashdod-Sfard's mind was racing. He felt a strong sense of exhilaration about having got rid of Haddley-Lassiter. "He won't turn over any of our other agents to the Iraqis," he thought. "Being a double agent is the most dangerous game, and Haddley-Lassiter finally got caught."

He picked up the telephone.

"I'd like to make a collect, person-to-person call, to Azazel Lekach, the editor of Shalom Books in Jerusalem." He gave the operator the phone number and waited for a few moments while the operator made the connection.

"He will accept your call," said the operator.

"Azazel," said Ashdod-Sfard. "How are you?"

"Fine," said Azazel. "Have you done any thinking about the title of that book you're working on?"

"Yes," said Ashdod-Sfard. "How about calling it *The Fall of a Sparrow*. It has a nice biblical ring to it."

"*Fall of a Sparrow*," said Azazel. "I rather like it. When did you come up with that title?"

"Yesterday," said Ashdod-Sfard. "In the evening. It was one of those ideas that seem to hit you over the head, if you know what I mean."

"Yes, I understand," said Azazel. "But watch out that you don't get a concussion. And how is the conference? Anything interesting to report? Any books we should think about translating? Any interesting scholars we might pursue with a publishing contract?"

"There's been some excitement," said Ashdod-Sfard. "It seems that Jean-Georg Simmul was murdered. We've put out a number of his books in my series. He was killed just a few minutes after he had given his presentation at our panel. I was about to introduce the next speaker, when the lights went out and there was chaos in the room. When they went on again, Simmul had a knife in his back. It was gruesome. I didn't like the man, and I know that he despised me, but it still was horrible to see what had happened to him."

"Have they found out who did it?" asked Azazel.

"Not yet. But I understand the police were snooping around and found a device with a timer somewhere in the hotel's electrical works. It was a professional job. There's reason to suspect that one of the panelists, Lisa Schauber Gurke, did it. There's a rumor about that she's a spy and knows a lot about how to manipulate electrical systems and that kind of thing."

"That's amazing! We we're thinking of translating one of her books," said Azazel. "I didn't know she was still around."

"Yes. She's getting old and seems very feeble. But it may be an act," responded Ashdod-Sfard. "There's more. It looks like Nigel Haddley-Lassiter, a British media scholar, committed suicide. Jumped out of a building. Terrible tragedy. The newspapers and television news shows are full of stuff about what's been going on here at the Hilton."

"I didn't know the man or his work, but I've heard of him," said Azazel. "He was a political scientist, wasn't he?"

"Yes," said Ashdod-Sfard. "He had the remarkable ability to write articles and books from, shall we say, both sides of an issue—or often more than just two sides. He called it being multidisciplinary; I called it being undisciplined. I've always thought, if you want to get to the truth of things, profound yourself in a discipline."

"Makes good sense to me," said Azazel.

"Azazel, I'll come and see you as soon as I return to Jerusalem. That will be in a few days. We can have lunch. Shalom."

"Shalom," said Azazel. "And be careful. San Francisco seems to be a very dangerous place. Watch yourself!"

Ashdod-Sfard looked out the window of his room, high above the city. It was in the middle of the morning. His mind started wandering and then racing about.

The fall of a sparrow. God is concerned with everything and everyone, the fall of a sparrow, the lives of the great and the small, and there is a season for all things, too. A time to live and a time to die. This was, it turns out, the time for Simmul to die. I can't understand why he despised me so much? It's hard to figure people out. He was a most intelligent man, but he also had a mean streak in him and often behaved in irrational ways. He probably harbored old grudges and was unwilling to give them up. That's tragic. We all have to be willing to forgive and to forget.

I had fantastic dreams last night. I dreamed that I was chased by a huge elephant through an enormous building, it had endlessly long corridors, huge windows, numerous patios. It was like those gigantic government buildings we have in Israel. I'd race down a hallway and go into a room, and then, suddenly, the elephant would break through a different door and eye me. No matter where I went the elephant would soon burst into the room.

"There's no escape, no escape," I thought. I ran into a large room that was full of people, thinking I could hide myself in the mass of humanity but then, to my dismay, the elephant raced in behind me and cornered me. It reared up on its hind legs, its snakelike trunk high in the air. I expected it would take me in its trunk and smash me against a wall or the floor, then I woke up, soaked in perspiration. I wonder what Freud would make of it? Or Jung? Is the dream some kind of archetype that is hard wired in us, somehow? Like people who feel they are drowning and can't get their breath? Is there a collective unconscious and is this dream connected to it? Do we get such dreams from the collective representations we are exposed to?

Collective representations are the result of an immense cooperation, which stretches out not only into space but into time as well: to make them, a multitude of minds have associated, united, and combined their ideas and sentiments; for them, long generations have accumulated their experience and their knowledge. A special intellectual activity is therefore concentrated in them that is infinitely richer and more complex than that of the individual. From that one can understand how the reason has been able to go beyond the limits of empirical knowledge.

It does not owe this to any vague mysterious virtue but simply to the fact that according to the well-known formula, man is double. There are two beings in him: an individual being, which has its foundation in the organism and the circle of whose activities is therefore strictly limited, and a social being, which represents the highest reality in the intellectual and moral order that we can know by observation—I mean society. This duality of our nature has as its consequence in the practical order, the

irreducibility of reason to individual experience. In so far as he belongs to society, the
individual transcends himself, both when he thinks and when he acts.

Someone told me a good joke yesterday. Very amusing.

A man comes home from work one day and sees his girlfriend packing her
suitcase. "What's going on?" he asks. "I'm leaving you," she says. "Why?" he
asks. "I've heard really terrible things about you from the neighbors," she answers.
"What did they say?" asks the man. "They say you're a pedophile!" "Hmph,"
says the man. "That's a pretty big word—for an eight-year-old!"

Why is this joke amusing? In part because it deals with the humor of exposure.
The man is revealed to be a pedophile. We are led astray by misunderstanding the
term girlfriend. We don't take it as literally as we should, thinking the term
girlfriend means "woman," since we are dealing with a man. In fact, the term
girlfriend is to be taken literally, an eight-year-old girl. We are also led astray by
the language the girlfriend uses: "I'm leaving you." That is the language conven-
tionally used by a woman who breaks up with a man. So we are played with by the
joke teller. We also recognize that the man is eccentric, at the least, and a moral
degenerate, at the most, since he is a pedophile. We learn this in the punch line
when he says that the term pedophile is a big word for an eight-year-old girl to
use. A most interesting joke. It deals with our sexuality, like many jokes. Curious
that we take something so important to us as our sexuality and make light of it, so
often, with humor. Perhaps because we all, men and women, the young and old,
feel anxiety-ridden and vulnerable when it comes to sex?

Curious, but nobody knows where jokes come from. Some people think Wall
Street brokers think them up when they have nothing better to do with their time.
Others say criminals do, but most criminals are too stupid to think up good jokes.
It takes a special kind of mind, no doubt about that. I've made a witty remark from
time to time; I've never thought up one actual joke. Maybe the people who think up
jokes start with a punch line and work backward? Some humorous material comes
from writers who think up clever dialogue for situation comedies and films, but
jokes—they're a different matter. Someone, somewhere thinks up a joke, and then,
of course, they tell that joke to friends, and then with the Internet, jokes now spread
all over the world in an instant. When we spread jokes by phones, people inadver-
tently put in slight variations of the jokes, but with e-mail, that doesn't happen so
much anymore. People can just forward the joke on to their friends.

I read Pavic's Dictionary of the Khazars recently. It was an interesting book.
The author tells a story three different ways—kind of like Rashomon, if you think
about it. And the book is modular, with many different segments and it is postmodern in that it has stories told within stories. I guess the secret of such novels is

finding a structure that will enable to the writer to do all kinds of things. The question about the book is whether it is comic or not. There is something comic about telling the story three different ways. You see how narrow and partial any one view of anything is. So even if it may have tragic elements in it, the book is ultimately comic, for it reveals what fools mortals are, as Puck would put it.

I wonder whether the novel, as we know it, will survive our new digiculture. Our electronic devices are getting smarter while, at the same time, people seem to be getting stupider. Where will it end? On the other hand, people love stories, and I can't imagine that anything will be able to replace the capacity of a written story to evoke, in the mind's eye, characters and situations. There are, after all, some things that can't be shown. And none of the computer programs that generate stories have done a very good job. The stories they create are garbage.

"God, I don't know what's happening to me," thought Ashdod-Sfard, as he slipped out of his daydream. "I find that my mind's been wandering a lot lately. Maybe it's time to retire and forget about all this academic nonsense. After all, what does it accomplish, in the final analysis? And I'm not getting any younger, either."

He looked at the table in his room where he had placed a small box of chocolates that someone had left for him.

"I think I could use some chocolate," he thought. "Chocolate is one of the few consolations we have to help us bear the pain of everyday life. One may be bored, one may suffer humiliations, one may have physical problems, one may has psychological problems, but there is always chocolate. I understand they've found that it actually helps people who are depressed and has antioxidants in it, so its good for people to help avoid getting cancer. Chocolate always makes me feel better, I know. I love its creamy texture, its sweetness, its complex flavors. Yes, chocolate has its virtues."

He walked over and picked up the box of chocolates, wrapped in a thin tan paper with the Godiva logo on it. Somebody had written a note, on a small card, in a delicate and flowery hand, "To Professor Elijah Ashdod-Sfard, who has done so much for the study of communication." It was signed, "A Secret Admirer."

"Hmm, I wonder who could have sent me these chocolates?" he thought. "Whoever it was, I really appreciate a most kind gesture. From a secret admirer—a touch of mystery, here." He started tearing off the cover of the box.

By "administrative" researchable problems we mean how to make an organization's actions more efficient, e.g., how best to advertise a brand of toothpaste, how most profitably to innovate word processors and video display terminals within a corporation, etc. By "critical" researchable problems we mean how to reshape or invent institutions to meet the collective needs of the relevant social community through devices such as direct broadcast satellites, terrestrial broadcast stations and networks, and cable TV, or, at a "micro" level, how to conduct psychotherapy and how to study rumors. By "administrative" tools, we refer to applications of a neopositivist, behavioral theory to the end of divining effects on *individuals*. By "critical" tools, we refer to historical, materialist analysis of the contradictory process in the real world. By "administrative" ideology, we mean the linking of administrative-type problems and tools, with interpretation of results that supports, or does not seriously disturb, the status quo. By "critical" ideology, we refer to the linking of "critical" researchable problems and critical tools with interpretations that involve radical changes in the established order.

—Dallas W. Smythe and Tran Van Dinh, "On Critical and Administrative Research: A New Critical Analysis," *Journal of Communication*, p. 118

THICK SMOKE WAS COMING OUT...

Just as Weems and Hunter were getting out of the elevator . . .

Just as Weems and Hunter were getting out of the elevator on the twenty-fourth floor of the Hilton, they heard a loud explosion.

"I'm pretty sure it came from Ashdod-Sfard's room," said Hunter. "It looks now like Simmul, even after his death, was able to figure out a way to kill him. Now we know what Simmul did with his bomb."

A siren in the hallway ceiling started blaring away. People in rooms near Ashdod-Sfard's had run into the hallway and were racing down the stairs, afraid of what might be coming next. Thick smoke was coming out from under the door of Ashdod-Sfard's room. Weems grabbed a fire extinguisher from the wall, and he and Hunter ran to the room.

"Watch out when I open the door, " said Hunter. "There'll be a blast of very hot air, so wait a minute."

He edged over to the door, inserted the plastic key, punched a button, and then, crouching against the wall, pushed it open with his foot. The room was full of smoke. The blast had broken the window in Ashdod-Sfard's room, and smoke was pouring out of it, also. Sirens from fire engines racing toward the Hilton could be heard.

After a couple of minutes, when the smoke had dissipated, they looked in the room. Ashdod-Sfard was dead. He'd been thrown into the bathroom by the explosion, and the room was a mass of blackened debris. Weems started spraying the room with foam from the fire extinguisher when some firefighters arrived on the scene.

"We'll take over," they said, carrying some powerful fire extinguishers. They used a walkie-talkie to communicate with a fire engine that was waiting below.

"We can take care of it," said one of the firefighters to someone below. "Looks like a small bomb went off. Did a hell of a lot of damage to the room but doesn't seem to have done any serious damage to the hotel. Have some folks take a look around, though. We don't want to take any chances."

They quickly doused the flames from the explosion.

"Jesus, what a mess," said one of the firefighters. "Looks like the guy blew himself up, or someone put a bomb in here and blew him up. It was a pretty powerful bomb."

"The person in this room was killed," said Hunter, "strange as it may seem, by someone who was murdered yesterday night. The person who was murdered sent something with a plastic bomb in it, before he was killed, to the victim here. This murder is the tragic conclusion to a cycle of murders that has taken place since last night. The killers were all professors on a panel at a conference here, and the victims were the other professors on the panel. There was a kind of murder-go-round here that started last night."

Weems had already pulled out his cell phone and had called headquarters. He chatted for a few moments with someone there.

"They were all spies, too," said Weems, turning to Hunter. "Our intelligence people just found out that Haddley-Lassiter was a spy; in fact, he was a double agent. It seems that he turned over the names of some Israeli agents in Iraq to the Iraqis. He didn't die from the fall, either. His head had been bashed in with a heavy object, and then someone—Ashdod-Sfard no doubt—pushed Haddley-Lassiter's body out of a window. In any case, a team will be here in a few minutes to take photos and take care of the body."

"There's no sense in remaining here," said Hunter. "Let's go back to headquarters, once the team arrives. I've got to get away from this place. It's a very sad commentary on human nature. Here we have a group of highly privileged people, who were also very intelligent and had positions of considerable prominence in the academic world. For one reason or another, whether it was because they nursed old grievances or had intense dislike for one another, each of the professors murdered someone else. They couldn't give up their hatred, and it destroyed them all."

Hunter finished explaining what happened to the firefighters.

"It all started when Lisa Schauber Gurke, an elderly professor from Germany, stuck a knife in the back of a famous professor from France, Jean-Georg Simmul. Gurke, in turn, was poisoned by a Russian professor, Mikhaila Blotnick-Kiev Vološinova, who was angry at Gurke because she had prevented Vološinova from getting a professorship at Harvard a number of years ago. Vološinova, in turn, was shot by a professor from England, Nigel Haddley-Lassiter, probably because she had seen him wearing women's clothes the night before and he was afraid she'd out him. He, in turn, had his head bashed in by Elijah Ashdod-Sfard, a professor from Israel. And Ashdod-Sfard was killed, in absentia, so to speak, by the already-dead Simmul, who had sent something to him with a bomb in it. Ashdod-Sfard, we believe, killed Haddley-Lassiter because he was a double agent who had double-crossed the Mossad.

"Curiously, they were all spies. Simmul worked for the Deuxième Bureau in France, Vološinova for OGPU, Sfard for Mossad, and Gurke for Stasi, which was located, before it was terminated, in East Germany. And Haddley-Lassiter worked for the Mossad and maybe a few other countries, as well—all at the same time.

"Probably it was their background in espionage that enabled them to accomplish some of the murders. Quite likely, Gurke—or an accomplice—did something to the electric system at the Hilton so it blacked out for a short while. That gave her time to stick a stiletto in Simmul's back. And it seems likely that Vološinova slipped some poison in something Gurke had to drink. It wouldn't be difficult."

"It sounds like a real massacre," said one of the firefighters. They

returned to the room to check on whether they'd completely extin-
guished the fire.

Hunter and Weems waited for the police team to arrive and then
returned to the station.

"Reminds me, Talcott," said Hunter, "of something I learned in a
chemistry class when I was in college, many, many years ago. One
day the professor came in and drew a picture of a snake with its tail
in its mouth. It's an old image that comes from Greece in the third
century before Christ. It seems that a German chemist, Kekule, who
was doing research into the molecular structure of benzene, had a
dream one night of that image of the snake with its tail in its mouth.
That led him to figure out the molecular structure of benzene, which
turns out to be a closed carbon ring.

"What happened here was similar in nature to the snake with its
tail in its mouth. It was, it turns out, a closed ring of murderers.
Snakes sometimes devour their young, and these professors
devoured each other. What a tragedy!"

"Could it be a comedy?" asked Weems. "The way each killer was,
in turn, murdered by another killer, has, I think, a kind of a black
comic element to it. The professors were all spies. There's something
comic about that, if you think about it. But the only one who killed
anyone because of all this spy business was Ashdod-Sfard, who killed
Haddley-Lassiter for being a double agent. The way these each of
these professors, who killed someone, became, in turn, a victim of
some other professor—that has, I think, a darkly comic touch to it.
And the fact that a dead professor, Simmul, killed a live one, is really
wild. It all strikes me as comic in that it shows what fools and self-
destructive idiots human beings can be. Even highly intelligent
idiots."

"I see what you mean," said Hunter. "Any death is a tragedy, but
when you look at the way these professors murdered one another, I
guess we could say that there is, actually, something comic about it
all. If it is a comedy, it's certainly not an ordinary one. It's a very dark
comedy, a very black one. Every killer was also a victim and every
victim was also a killer."

"What are you going to call this case?" asked Weems.

"I think I'll call it 'The Mass Comm Murders,' " Hunter replied.

"How does that sound? These professors were experts on mass communications. Too bad they didn't know more about interpersonal communication and didn't have enough heart to forgive and forget. It may be some kind of a bizarre comedy, Talcott, but I also think it's a very sad story."

Questions for Discussion

In answering these questions, please make sure to support your assertions and opinions with reasons, evidence, facts, and so forth, that a fair-minded person would find acceptable.

1. In the DeFleur and Ball-Rokeach selection, there are five attacks and six defenses of the media. Which attacks do you think are reasonable? Which defenses strike you as valid? Which side do you think is most correct? Why?

2. How would you define stereotypes? What stereotypes of Russian women are made? What's wrong with these stereotypes? If stereotypes of Russian men were made, how would they have differed from the ones made of the women?

3. Simmul describes America as being a consumption culture. What is a consumption culture? Is there anything wrong with being a consumption culture? What other kinds of cultures are there?

4. Is Simmul's "motelization theory" correct? Do his theories about freezers, white bread, and status in foods make sense? What about his modest proposal? How would you describe Simmul's ideas? What is he trying to do in his lecture?

5. Tony Schwartz suggests that we become programmed by the media and then can be "turned on" by the correct stimulus. What do you think of this notion? Support your opinion with reasons.

6. Contrast the hypodermic needle theory of mass communication with the reader-response theory. Which seems most correct or are both wrong? Do you have an alternative theory? Support your answer with reasons.

7. Haddley-Lassister argues that theory is important for all research,

that it is the "driving force" behind research, and everything else is secondary. What do you think of this idea? Why? How do you explain the way scholars and others become fascinated by "theory"?

8. Haddley-Lassiter attacks Simmul on a number of different grounds. Discuss his reasons for criticizing Simmul. What do you think of them?

9. Explain Vološinova's "dialogic" theory in as much detail as you can. What do you think of it? Are there alternative theories you can think of that do a better job of explaining communication? If so, what are they?

10. Ashdod-Sfard argues that there is really no such thing as a discipline called communication. Explain his argument about this matter, his theory about the spiral of silence, and his other notions about media. Evaluate them and justify your opinions.

11. William McGuire offers a number of reasons for arguing the media are weak and that the media are strong. Which arguments seems to be most convincing to you? What do you think—are the media weak or strong? Defend your position with reasons.

12. Explain Gurke's theory of media events. What is a media event? Why are media events significant? What do you think are some of the most important media events since 1990?

13. Discuss Gurke's theory of "uses and gratifications." What's the difference between a "use" and a "gratification"? Can you think of other media uses and gratifications besides the ones she lists? If so, what are they?

14. Robert Sholes argues that "the message itself, uniting sender and receiver, in the quintessentially human act of communication, is simply a verbal form, which depends on all the other elements of a speech event to convey its meaning. *The message is not the meaning.*" What is the message, not the meaning? What points is he making? Do you agree with him? Justify your answer with reasons.

15. Explain Marshall McLuhan's theory about hot and cold media and evaluate it, giving reasons for your position. List as many hot and cold media (as polar opposites) as you can think of.

16. Professor Gurke has some notions about the significance of the

television show *Survivor*. What are her ideas? How valid are they? Do you have other explanations for the popularity of the show?

17. Karl Mannheim in his work on the sociology of knowledge argues that "strictly speaking it is incorrect to say that the single individual thinks. Rather it is more correct to insist that he participates in thinking further what other men have thought before him." What do you think of this idea? If he is correct, how do we get new ideas?

18. Professor Vološinova's journal contains a number of ideas and judgments. Discuss her ideas and evaluate her judgments about universities, men, professors, Albert Fess and malls, and sociology.

19. Discuss and evaluate the theory about "gatekeeping." Justify your opinions. Who are the gatekeepers now? Has the Internet changed things as far as gatekeeping is concerned?

20. Describe in detail and evaluate the theories found in Haddley-Lassiter's book proposal. Does the theory of "vicious cycles" seem correct? If so, why? If not, why not? What about the theories about audiences and rhetoric? If you were editing the book, what theories would you add to the proposal?

21. Ashdod-Sfard meditates about collective representations. What do you think of the concept? How does it help explain individual choice despite the power of mass media?

Glossary

Aberrant decoding. The notion that audiences interpret (i.e., decode) texts in ways that differ from the ways the creators of these texts had expected them to be decoded. Aberrant decoding is the rule, rather than the exception, when it comes to the mass media, according to the semiotician Umberto Eco.

Administrative research. This research focuses on ways of making communication by organizations and other entities more effective and more efficient. It uses statistics and other empirical means of collecting data. It contrasts with critical research, which has more of an interest in culture, social justice, and related considerations.

Agenda setting. According to this theory, the various kinds of mass communication don't determine what we think but do play a major role in determining what we think about. This involves both what the media present to us and how they present it. In effect, the media set an agenda for our decision making and thus influence public debate about our social and political life.

Attitudes. An attitude, as social psychologists use the term, refers to a relatively long-lasting state of mind in a person about some phenomenon or aspect of experience. Attitudes generally are either positive or negative, have direction, and involve thoughts, feelings, and behaviors (tied to these attitudes).

Audience. Audiences are generally understood to be collections of individuals who watch a television program, listen to a radio program, or attend a film or some kind of artistic performance (symphony, ballet, rock concert, etc.). The members of the audience may be together in one room or scattered, or, in the case of television, they can be individuals, each watching from his or her own set. In technical terms, audiences are addressees who receive mediated texts sent by some addresser.

Broadcast. We use the term to deal with texts that are made available over wide areas by using radio or television signals. Broadcasting differs from other forms of distributing texts such as cablecasting, which uses cables, and satellite transmission, which requires "dishes" to capture signals sent by the satellites.

Class. From a linguistic standpoint, a class is any group of things that has something in common. We use it to refer to social classes or, more literally, socioeconomic classes: groups of people who differ in terms of income and lifestyle. Marxist theorists argue that there is a ruling class that owns and controls the media and thus shapes the ideas of the proletariat, the working classes.

Codes. Codes are systems of symbols, letters, words, sounds, whatever, that generate meaning. Language, for example, is a code. It uses combinations of letters that we call words to mean certain things. The relation between the word and the thing the word stands for is arbitrary, based on convention. In some cases, the term *code* is used to describe hidden meanings and disguised communications.

Cognitive dissonance. The term *dissonance* refers to sounds that clash with one another. According to psychologists, people wish to avoid ideas that challenge the ones they hold, which create conflict and other disagreeable feelings. Cognitive dissonance refers to ideas that conflict with ones people hold and generate psychological anxiety and displeasure.

Collective representations. The French sociologist Emile Durkheim used this concept to deal with the fact that people are both individuals, pursuing their own aims, and social animals, who are guided by the groups and societies in which they find themselves. Collective representations are, broadly speaking, texts that reflect the beliefs and ideals of groups and other collectivities.

Communication. There are many different ways of understanding and using this term. For our purposes, communication is a process that involves the transmission of messages from senders to receivers. We often make a distinction between communication using language—verbal communication—and communication using facial expressions, body language, and other means—nonverbal communication.

Communications. The plural of the term refers to what is communicated in contrast to the process of communication, described earlier.

Concept. We will understand concept to be a general idea or notion that explains or helps us understand some phenomenon or phenomena. I make a distinction between theories and concepts. Theories employ concepts. Thus, Freudian theory makes use of concepts such as id, ego, and superego.

Consumer cultures. Capitalist societies whose economies are based on mass production and widespread consumption of objects and services are held to be consumer cultures. Advertising plays a major role in stimulating consumption in such societies. Some Marxists argue that capitalism can generate consumption but also creates alienation and that mass consumption represents an unconscious attempt by people to deal with the pain of alienation.

Contact. In Roman Jakobson's theory, the contact is the medium through which the message is passed from the sender to the receiver.

Content analysis. A methodology for obtaining statistical data from a collection of texts that are similar in some respect. Content analysis is a nonintrusive way of conducting research.

Critical research. This term refers to approaches to the media that are essentially ideological, that focus on the social and political dimensions of the mass media and the way they are used by organizations and others allegedly to maintain the status quo rather than enhancing equality. Critical research contrasts with administrative research, which focuses on the efficient use of media by organizations and other entities.

Cultivation theory. This theory argues that television dominates the symbolic environment of its audiences and gives people false views of what reality is like. That is, television "cultivates" or reinforces certain beliefs in its viewers, such as the notion that society is permeated by violence, that there are hardly any older people, and so on.

Cultural homogenization. The term *cultural homogenization* refers to the theory that the media of mass communication, which are generally created by first world societies, are destroying third world cultures and regional cultures in specific countries, leading to a cultural sameness, standardization, or "homogenization."

Cultural imperialism (also media imperialism). This theory describes the flow of media products (e.g., films and television programs) and popular culture from the United States and a few other capitalist countries in Western Europe to the third world and argues that this flow is leading to cultural homogenization and the dominance of bourgeois capitalist values. Along with these texts and popular culture, it is alleged that values and beliefs (and bourgeois capitalist ideology) are also being transmitted, leading to the domination of these people.

Culture. Generally speaking, from the anthropological perspective culture involves the transmission from generation to generation, by various means, of specific ideas, arts, customary beliefs, ways of living, behavior patterns, institutions, and values. When applied to the arts, culture generally is used to specify so-called elite kinds of art works, such as operas, poetry, classical music, serious novels, and the like. Popular culture refers to mass-mediated kinds of "low" art such as television commercials, television programs, most films, genre works of literature, and popular music.

Defense mechanisms. These are methods used by the ego, the mediating element in the psyche, to defend itself against pressures from id or impulsive elements in the psyche and superego elements such as conscience and guilt. Some of the more common defense mechanisms are repression (barring unconscious instinctual wishes, memories, etc., from consciousness), regression (returning to earlier stages in one's development), ambivalence (a simultaneous feeling of love and hate for some person), and rationalization (offering excuses to justify one's actions).

Demographics. This term refers to similarities found in selected groups of people in terms of matters such as race, religion, gender, social class, ethnicity, occupation, place of residence, and age.

Deviance. This concept refers to groups of people and individuals whose values and beliefs and behavior patterns are different (i.e., deviate from) from those of most people in society. At one time *deviant* had a negative connotation, but in recent years it has come to mean "different," but not necessarily "bad."

Dialogism. This theory, elaborated by the Russian Mikhail Bakhtin, argues that communication is best understood as being like dialogue—that is, it is interactive. Thus, communication is affected by what has been previously communicated and what communicators expect will be communicated to them in the future.

Disfunctional (also dysfunctional). In sociological thought, something is disfunctional if it contributes to the breakdown or destabilization of the entity in which it is found.

Ego. In Freud's theory of the psyche, the ego functions as the executant of the id and as a mediator between the id and the superego. The ego is involved with the perception of reality and the adaptation to reality.

Emotive functions. According to the linguist Roman Jakobson, messages have a number of functions. One of the most important of them is the emotive function, which involves expressing feelings by the sender of a message. (Other functions are referential and poetic.)

Empiricism. This theory argues that social scientists should strive for objectivity and deal, as much as possible, with material that is observable, that can be measured, and that can be quantified.

Ethnocentrism. This term refers to the notion held by some members of some ethnic groups that their ideas, their customs, their beliefs, and their way of life are better than those of other ethnic groups. Ethnocentrism is often based on stereotyped thinking.

False consciousness. In Marxist theory, false consciousness refers to mistaken ideas or illusions that people have about matters such as their class, their status, and their economic possibilities. These illusions help maintain the status quo and are of great use to the ruling class, which wants to avoid changes in the social structure. Marx argued that the ideas of the masses are always those of the ruling classes.

Feminist criticism. There are many kinds of feminist criticism. As a rule, it focuses on the roles given to women and the way they are portrayed in general in mass mediated texts of all kinds, with a particular focus on advertising and literary, film, and television narratives. Feminist critics claim that women are typically used essentially as sexual objects and are portrayed stereotypically in texts, and these portrayals have destructive effects on women and also on men. Feminists argue that most societies are "phallocentric," dominated in subtle ways by the male phallus.

Formula. A formula in narrative theory refers to a text with conventional characters and actions with which audiences are familiar. Genre texts, such as detective stories, westerns, science fiction adventures, and romances, are highly formulaic, while elite texts, such as James Joyce's *Ulysses*, are held to be innovative and nonformulaic.

Functional. Sociologists use the term *functional* to refer to the contribution an institution makes to the maintenance and continuation of a society. An institution is functional if it helps maintain the system in which it is found; it is disfunctional if it contributes to the breakdown of the system in which it is found, and it is nonfunctional if it plays no role of any consequence in the system in which it is found.

Functional alternative. The term *functional alternative* refers to something that is an alternative to something—that is, it takes the place of something else. For example, professional football can be seen as a functional alternative to religion.

Gatekeepers. Gatekeepers are those who determine what stories are used in magazines, newspapers, or news programs on the electronic media. Literally speaking, a gatekeeper is someone who stands at some gate and determines who or what goes through it. Thus, gatekeepers determine what news stories we get but, in a broader sense, what television programs we watch and what films we see, what songs we hear, and so on.

Genre. The term *genre* is French and means "kind" or "class." In popular usage,

120

it refers to the kind of formulaic texts found in the mass media. For example, on television we find genres such as talk shows, news shows, sports programs, sitcoms, action adventure programs, horror shows, detective programs, and commercials.

Hot and cold media. Marshall McLuhan argued that hot media are characterized by high definition (much data) and low participation, while cool media are characterized by low definition (little data) and high participation. For McLuhan, radio, movies, photographs, and the printed word are hot media, and the telephone, television, cartoons, and speech are cool media.

Hypodermic needle theory of media. The hypodermic needle theory, now generally discredited, asserts that all members of an audience "read" or "decode" a text the same way and get the same things out of it. Media are seen like a hypodermic needle, injecting their message to one and all.

Hypothesis. A hypothesis is a notion or idea that is assumed to be true for the purposes of discussion or argument or further investigation. That is, a hypothesis is, in a sense, a guess or supposition that is used to explain some phenomenon.

Id. In Freud's theory of the psyche (technically known as his structural hypothesis), the id is that element of the psyche that is the representative of a person's drives. Freud described it, in his *New Introductory Lectures on Psychoanalysis*, as "a chaos, a cauldron of seething excitement." The id also is the source of energy, but since it lacks direction, it needs the ego to harness it and control it. In popular thought, it is connected with impulse, lust, and "I want it all now" kind of behavior.

Ideology. An ideology is generally understood to be to a logically coherent, integrated explanation of social, economic, and political matters that helps establish the goals and direct the actions of some group or political entity. People act or don't act (and vote or don't vote) on the basis of some ideology they hold, even though they may not have articulated it or thought about it.

Image. I define an image in my book *Seeing Is Believing: An Introduction to Visual Communication* (Mayfield, 1998: 45) as "a collection of signs and symbols—what we find when we look at a photograph, a film still, a shot of a television screen, a print advertisement, or just about anything." The term is also used for mental as well as physical representations of things. Images often have powerful emotional effects on people and historical significance, as, for example, the televised images on 11 September 2001 of planes crashing into the World Trade Center.

Lasswell formula. In 1948 the political scientist Harold Lasswell started an article by writing:

A convenient way to describe an act of communication is to answer the following questions:
Who?
Says what?
In which channel?
To whom?
With what effect?
This is probably the most famous phrase ever uttered in mass communication theory.

Latent functions. Sociologists distinguish between latent and manifest functions. Latent functions are the hidden, unrecognized, and unintended functions of some activity, entity, or institution. They are the opposite, then, of manifest functions, which are recognized and intended.

Lifestyles. This term means, literally, "style of life." It refers to the way people live—to the decisions they make about such matters as how to decorate their apartment or home (and where it is located), the make and style of cars they drive, the clothes they wear, the kinds of foods they eat and the restaurants they go to, the pets they have, and where they go for vacations.

Limited effects (of media). A number of mass communication theorists claim that the mass media have relatively minor effects in the scheme of things. They cite research that suggests, for example, that effects from media don't tend to be long-lasting and argue that the notion that mass media have strong and long-lasting effects has not been demonstrated.

Manifest functions. Manifest functions, sociologists tell us, are those functions that are obvious and intended. Manifest functions thus contrast with latent functions, which are hidden and unintended. The manifest function of joining a sorority may be to find housing, while the latent function might be to be able to move in the right circles to find suitable marriage mates.

Mass. For our purposes, the term *mass* as in "mass communication" refers to a large number of people who are the audience for some communication. There is considerable disagreement about how to understand this term. Some media theorists say it is composed of individuals who are heterogeneous, do not know one another, do not have a leader, and are alienated. Others attack these notions, saying they are not based on fact or evidence but on theories that have not been substantiated.

Mass communication. *Mass communication* refers to the transfer of messages, information, texts, and the like from a sender of some kind to a large number of receivers—that is, people who form a large audience. This transfer is done through the technologies of the mass media—newspapers, magazines, television programs, films, records, computers, CD-ROMs, and so on. The sender often is a person in some large media organization, the messages are public, and the audience tends to be large and varied.

Media effects. That branch of mass communication theory that focuses its attention on the short-term and long-term effects of media on people. Some theorists argue that the media are very powerful and have strong effects, while others argue that the media are not powerful and have weak effects.

Media events. A media event is one that is either planned or unplanned and has global significance—such as the marriage of Queen Elizabeth or the destruction of the World Trade Center. These events attract the attention of media from all over the world and are watched by hundreds of millions of people all over the world.

Medium (plural: media). A medium is understood to be a means of delivering messages, information, and various kinds of texts to audiences. There are different ways of classifying the media. Some of the most common are: print (newspapers, magazines, books, billboards), electronic (radio, television, computers, CD-ROMs), and photographic (photographs, films, videos).

Metaphor. Metaphors are figures of speech that convey meanings by analogy. It is important to realize that metaphors are not confined to poetry and literary works but, according to some linguists, are the fundamental way in which we make sense of things and find meaning in the world. A simile is a weak form of metaphor that uses either *like* or *as* in making an analogy. "My love is a rose" is a metaphor; "My love is like a rose" is a simile.

Metonymy. According to linguists, metonymy is a figure of speech that conveys information by association and is, along with metaphor, one of the most important ways people convey information to one another. We tend not to be aware of our use of metonymy, but whenever we use association to get an idea about something (Rolls-Royce = wealthy), we are thinking metonymically. A form of metonymy that involves seeing a whole in terms of a part or vice versa is called *synecdoche*. Using "The Pentagon" to stand for the American military establishment is an example of synecdoche.

Model. In the social sciences, models are held to be abstract representations that show how some generally complicated phenomenon functions. Theories are typically expressed in language, but models tend to be represented graphically in diagrams along with by statistics or mathematical formulations. Denis McQuail and Sven Windahl define *model* in *Communication Models for the Study of Mass Communication* (Longman, 1993: 2) as "a consciously simplified description in graphic form of a piece of reality. A model seeks to show the main elements of any structure or process and the relationships between these elements."

Modernism. This term is used in criticism to deal with the arts in the period from approximately the turn of the twentieth century until about the 1960s. The modernists rejected narrative structure for simultaneity and montage and explored the paradoxical nature of reality. Some of the more important modernists were T. S. Eliot, Franz Kafka, James Joyce, Pablo Picasso, Henri Matisse, and Eugene Ionesco. The modernists set the stage, certain theorists argue, for the period that comes after modernism—namely, postmodernism.

Narrowcasting. A medium like radio that has stations that tend to focus on discrete groups of people is said to be narrowcasting.

Nonfunctional. In sociological thought, something is nonfunctional if it is neither functional nor disfunctional but plays no role in the entity in which it is found.

Nonverbal communication. Nonverbal communication involves such matters as our body language, facial expressions, style of dress, and style of wearing our hair. These matters are ways for us to communicate our feelings and attitudes (and a sense of who we are) without using words.

Opinion leader. This term refers to those people whose opinions affect the opinions of others, who follow their lead, so to speak. The notion that there are opinion leaders is part of the two-step flow theory of communication.

Phallic symbol. In Freudian psychoanalytic theory, any object that resembles the penis by either shape or function is described as a phallic symbol. Symbolism is a defense mechanism of the ego that permits hidden or repressed sexual or aggressive thoughts to be expressed in a disguised form. For a more complete discussion of this topic, see Freud's book *An Interpretation of Dreams*.

Phallocentric. Feminist theorists and others us this term is used to suggest that societies are dominated by males and that the ultimate source of this domination, that which shapes our institutions and cultures, is the male phallus. In this theory, a link is made between male sexuality and male power.

Poetic functions. In Roman Jakobson's theory, poetic functions are those that use literary devices such as metaphor and metonymy. Poetic functions differ, Jakobson suggests, from emotive functions and referential functions.

Popular. Popular is one of the most difficult and controversial terms used in discourse about the arts and the media. Literally speaking, the term means appealing to large number of people. It comes from the Latin term *popularis*, "of the people." Some media theorists argue that for something to be popular, it must be of low quality.

Popular culture. This term identifies certain kinds of texts that are generally carried by the mass media and are designed to appeal to large numbers of people. But mass communication theorists often identify (or some would say confuse) "popular" with "mass" and suggest that if something is popular, it must be of poor quality, appealing to the mythical "lowest common denominator." Popular culture is generally held to be the opposite of "elite" culture—arts that require certain levels of sophistication and refinement to be appreciated, such as ballet, opera, poetry, and classical music. Many critics now question this popular culture/elite culture polarity.

Postmodernism. Some theorists suggest that we are all living in a postmodern era—and have been doing this since the 1960s, more or less. Literally speaking, the term means "coming after" modernism, the period from approximately 1900 to the 1960s. Postmodernism is characterized by—as a leading theorist of the subject, Jean-François Lyotard, put it—"incredulity toward metanarratives" (*The Postmodern Condition: A Report on Knowledge*, University of Minnesota Press, 1984: xxiv). By this he suggests that the old philosophical belief systems that had helped people order their lives and societies no longer are accepted or given credulity. This leads to a period in which, some argue, anything goes.

Pragmatic theory of art. This theory of art holds that art must do something, have certain consequences that are held to be desirable. Thus, art should teach or indoctrinate or perform some function.

Psychoanalytic theory. Psychoanalytic theory is based on the notion that the human psyche has what Freud called the "unconscious," which is inaccessible to us, ordinarily speaking (unlike consciousness and the preconscious), and which continually shapes and affects our mental functioning and behavior. We can symbolize Freud's ideas by imagining an iceberg: The tip of the iceberg, which shows above the water, represents consciousness. This tip is only a small part of the iceberg. The part of the iceberg we can see just below the surface of the water represents the preconscious. And the rest of iceberg (i.e., most of it) represents the unconscious. We cannot access this hidden area of our psyches because of repression. Freud also emphasized matters such as sexuality and the role of the Oedipus complex in everyone's lives.

Psychographics. Marketers use this term to deal with groups of people who have similar psychological characteristics or profiles. It differs from demographics, which marketers use to focus on social and economic characteristics that some people have in common.

Public. Instead of the term *popular culture*, we sometimes use the terms *the public arts* or *public communication* to avoid the negative connotations of *mass* and *popular*. A public is a group of people, a community. We can contrast public acts—those meant to be known to the community—with private acts, which are not meant to be known to others.

Rationalization. In Freudian psychoanalytic thought, a rationalization is one of the defense mechanisms of the ego that creates some excuse or excuses to justify some action (or inaction when an action is expected). Ernest Jones, who introduced the term, used it to describe logical and rational reasons that people give to justify behavior that is really caused by unconscious and irrational determinants.

Reader response theory (also reception theory). This theory suggests that readers (a term used very broadly to cover people who read books, watch television programs, go to films, listen to texts on the radio, etc.) play an important role in the realization of texts. Texts, then, function as sites for the creation of meaning by readers, and different readers, based on their histories, beliefs, and knowledge, interpret a given text differently.

Referential functions. In Roman Jakobson's theory, the referential function of speech deals with the way it helps speakers relate to their surroundings. He contrasts this with emotive and poetic functions of speech.

Repetition compulsion. Freud explained repetition compulsion as the need to repeat earlier experiences, generally of a painful nature, to help one's psyche deal with them and achieve a measure of psychological closure on them.

Ritual. Ritual is to be understood as a highly structured, symbolically significant mode or pattern of behavior, often with religious significance. In some cases, in the case of people with obsessive compulsive personality types, endlessly repeated rituals dominate their everyday life.

Selective attention (or selective inattention). According to this theory, we have a tendency to avoid messages that conflict with our beliefs and values and cause cognitive dissonance. One way we do this is by selective attention—by avoiding or not paying attention to messages that would generate this dissonance.

Semiotics. *Semiotics* means, literally speaking, "the science of signs." *Semion* is the Greek term for "sign." A sign is anything that can be used to stand for anything else. According to C. S. Peirce, one of the founders of the science, a sign "is something which stands to somebody for something in some respect or capacity."

Serial texts. Texts that continue on for long periods of time are called serial texts. Good examples would be comics, soap operas, and other television narratives that are on for extended periods of time. Serial texts pose problems for critics: what is the text, and how do we deal with it?

Simulation. This term, made popular by the French philosopher Jean Baudrillard, refers to the notion that images often bear no relation to the reality they are meant to portray and that signs take on their own life. As Baudrillard has written in his book *Simulations* (Semiotext(e)/Autonomedia, 1983: 2), "simulation is no longer that of a territory; a referential being or a substance. It is the generation by models of a real world without origins or reality: a hyperreal."

Socialization. This term refers to the processes by which societies teach individuals how to behave: what rules to obey, roles to assume, and values to hold. Socialization was traditionally done by the family, educators, religious figures, and peers. The mass media seem to have usurped this function to a considerable degree nowadays, with consequences that are not always positive.

Socioeconomic class. This is a categorization of people according to their incomes and related social status and lifestyles. In Marxist thought, there are ruling classes that shape the consciousness of the working classes, and history is, in essence, a record of class conflict. Many Americans believe the United States is a classless, all middle-class society, but in reality it has many different socioeconomic classes.

Sociology of knowledge. This theory argues that the societies in which we are born and grow up help shape our ideas about ourselves and the world. That is, we have to consider the social origins of knowledge. Our thinking is always based, to a degree, on the thoughts and ideas of others who have preceded us.

Spiral of silence. This theory, developed by Elizabeth Noelle-Neumann, holds that people with views that they think are not popular tend to keep quiet, while those who have views that they believe are widely accepted tend to state them very strongly. This leads to a spiral in which certain views tend to be suppressed while others gain increased prominence. The views of minorities are held to be weaker than they actually are, and the views of majorities are perceived as stronger than they actually are.

Stereotypes. Stereotypes are generally defined as commonly held, simplistic, and inaccurate group portraits of categories of people. While stereotypes can be positive, negative, or mixed, generally they are negative in nature. Stereotyping always involves making gross overgeneralizations. All Mexicans, Chinese, Arabs, Jews, African Americans, WASPs, Americans, lawyers, doctors, professors, and so on, are held to have certain characteristics, usually something negative.

Subculture. We use the term *subculture* to refer to cultural subgroups whose religion, ethnicity, sexual orientation, beliefs, values, behaviors, and life-styles vary in certain ways from those of the dominant culture. In any complex society, it is normal to have a considerable number of subcultures.

Superego. According to Freud, the superego is the agency in our psyches related to conscience and morality. The superego is involved with processes such as approval and disapproval of wishes on the basis or whether they are moral, critical self-observation, and a sense of guilt over wrongdoing. These functions of the superego are largely unconscious and are opposed to id elements in our psyches. Mediating between the two, and trying to balance them, are our egos.

Text. For our purposes, a text is, broadly speaking, any work of art in any medium. Critics use the term *text* as a convenience—so they don't have to name a given work all the time or use various synonyms. There are problems involved in deciding what the text is when we deal with serial texts, such as soap operas or comics.

Theory. Theories are expressed in language and systematically and logically attempt to explain and predict phenomena being studied. Theories differ from concepts, which define phenomena that are being studied, and from models, which are abstract, usually graphic in nature, and explicit about what is being studied.

Two-step flow. This refers to a theory of how mass communication reaches and affects people. According to this theory, in the first step, the media influence opinion leaders; in the second step, the opinion leaders influence others.

Uses and gratifications. This theory argues that researchers should pay attention to the way audiences use the media (or certain texts or genres of texts) and the gratifications they get from their use of these texts and the media. Uses and gratification researchers focus their attention, then, on how audiences use the media rather than how the media affect audiences.

Values. Values are abstract and general beliefs or judgments about what is right and wrong, what is good and bad, that have implications for individual behavior and for social, cultural, and political entities. There are a number of problems with values from a philosophical point of view. First, how does one determine which values are correct or good and which aren't? That is, how do we justify values? Are values objective or subjective? Second, what happens when there is a conflict between groups, each of which holds central values that conflict with those of a different group?

Vicious cycles. This theory argues that media such as television often create anxieties in young people who watch programs that are too adult for them.

This leads to various problems they have when they are older. Ironically, they then use the media to help them deal with the very problems the media created.

Youth culture. Youth cultures are defined as subcultures formed by young people around some area of life of great interest, usually connected with leisure, entertainment, and consumer culture, such as rock music or some aspect of computers, such as games and hacking. Typically youth cultures adopt distinctive ways of dressing and develop institutions that cater to their needs.

Bibliography

Note: Books by fictional characters are in bold print.

Abelove, Henry, Michele A. Barale, and David Halperin, eds. 1993. *The Lesbian and Gay Studies Reader*. New York: Routledge.

Adorno, Theodor W. 1991. *The Culture Industry: Selected Essays on Mass Culture*. London: Routledge.

Aitken, Stuart C., and Leo E. Zonn. 1994. *Place, Power, Situation and Spectacle: A Geography of Film*. Lanham, Md.: Rowman & Littlefield.

Aronowitz, Stanley. 1993. *Dead Artists, Live Theories and Other Cultural Problems*. New York: Routledge.

Ashdod-Sfard, Elijah. *The Cycle of Silence*. Jerusalem: Luftmensch.

Atkin, Charles, and Lawrence Wallack. 1992. *Mass Communication and Public Health*. Thousand Oaks, Calif.: Sage.

Bakhtin, M. M. 1981. *The Dialogic Imagination*. Trans. Caryl Emerson and Michael Holmquist; ed. Michael Holmquist. Austin: University of Texas Press.

———. 1984. *Rabelais and His World*. Trans. Helene Iswolsky. Bloomington: Indiana University Press.

Bal, Mieke. 1985. *Narratology: Introduction to the Theory of Narrative*. Toronto: University of Toronto Press.

Barker, Martin, and Ann Beezer. 1992. *Reading into Cultural Studies*. London: Routledge.

Barthes, Roland. 1972. *Mythologies*. Trans. Annette Lavers. New York: Hill & Wang.

———. 1975. *The Pleasure of the Text*. Trans. Richard Miller. New York: Hill & Wang.

———. 1977. *Empire of Signs*. Trans. Stephen Heath. New York: Hill & Wang.

———. 1988. *The Semiotic Challenge*. Trans. Richard Howard. New York: Hill & Wang.

130   BIBLIOGRAPHY

Baudrillard, Jean. 1983. *Simulations*. Trans. Paul Foss, et al. New York: Semio-
text(e).
————. 1994. *Symbolic Exchange and Death*. Trans. Ian Grant. Thousand Oaks,
Calif.: Sage.
Bennett, Tony, and Janet Woollacott. 1987. *Bond and Beyond: The Political Career
of a Popular Hero*. New York: Methuen.
Berger, Arthur Asa. 1990. *Agitpop: Political Culture and Communication Theory*. New
Brunswick, N.J.: Transaction.
————. 1994a. *Blind Men and Elephants: Perspectives on Humor*. New Brunswick,
N.J.: Transaction.
————. 1994b. *Cultural Criticism: A Primer of Key Concepts*. Thousand Oaks, Calif.:
Sage.
————. 1997. *Postmortem for a Postmodernist*. Walnut Creek, Calif.: AltaMira.
————. 1999a. *Media Analysis Techniques*. 2d ed. Thousand Oaks, Calif.: Sage.
————. 1999b. *Signs in Contemporary Culture: An Introduction to Semiotics*. 2d ed.
Salem, Wisc.: Sheffield.
————. 2000. *Ads, Fads and Consumer Culture*. Lanham, Md.: Rowman & Little-
field.
————. 2001. *Video Games: A Popular Culture Phenomenon*. Piscataway, N.J.: Trans-
action.
Berman, Marshall. 1982. *All That Is Solid Melts into Air: The Experience of Modernity*.
New York: Touchstone.
Best, Steven, and Douglas Kellner. 1991. *Postmodern Theory*. New York: Guilford.
Bettelheim, Bruno. 1976. *The Uses of Enchantment*. New York: Knopf.
Bhabha, Homi. 1993. *Location of Culture*. New York: Routledge.
Blau, Herbert. 1992. *To All Appearances: Ideology and Performance*. London:
Routledge.
Bogart, Leo. 1985. *Polls and the Awareness of Public Opinion*. New Brunswick, N.J.:
Transaction.
Bourdieu, Pierre. 1994. *Sociology in Question*. Trans. Richard Nice. Thousand
Oaks, Calif.: Sage.
Bowlby, Rachel. 1993. *Shopping with Freud: Items on Consumerism, Feminism and Psy-
choanalysis*. London: Routledge.
Bramson, Leon. 1961. *The Political Context of Sociology*. Princeton, N.J.: Princeton
University Press.
Branigan, Edward. 1992. *Narrative Comprehension and Film*. New York: Routledge.
Brown, Mary Ellen, ed. 1990. *Television and Women's Culture: The Politics of the Popu-
lar*. Newbury Park, Calif.: Sage.
————. 1994. *Soap Opera and Woman's Talk: The Pleasure of Resistance*. Thousand
Oaks, Calif.: Sage.

Buckley, F. H. 2001. *The Morality of Laughter*. Piscataway, N.J.: Transaction.

Buck-Morss, Susan. 1989. *The Dialectics of Seeing: Walter Benjamin and the Arcades Project*. Minneapolis: University of Minnesota Press.

Butler, Judith. 1993. *Bodies That Matter*. New York: Routledge.

Cantor, Muriel G. 1988. *The Hollywood TV Producer*. New Brunswick, N.J.: Transaction.

Cantor, Muriel G., and Joel M. Cantor. 1991. *Prime-Time Television: Content and Control*. Thousand Oaks, Calif.: Sage.

Carey, James, ed. 1987. *Media, Myths and Narratives: Television and the Press*. Newbury Park, Calif.: Sage.

Certeau, Michel de. 1984. *The Practice of Everyday Life*. Trans. Steven Rendall. Berkeley: University of California Press.

———. 1986. *Heterologies: Discourse on the Other*. Trans. Brian Massumi. Minneapolis: University of Minnesota Press

Clarke, John. 1992. *New Times and Old Enemies: Essays on Cultural Studies and America*. London: Routledge.

Collins, Jim, Hillary Radner, and Ava Preacher Collins, eds. 1992. *Film Theory Goes to the Movies: Cultural Analysis of Contemporary Film*. New York: Routledge.

Collins, Richard, James Curran, Nicholas Garnham, and Paddy Scannell, eds. 1986. *Media, Culture & Society: A Critical Reader*. Newbury Park, Calif.: Sage.

Combs, James. E. 2000. *Play World: The Emergence of a New Ludenic Age*. Westport, Conn.: Greenwood.

Crane, Diane. 1992. *The Production of Culture: Media and the Urban Arts*. Newbury Park, Calif.: Sage.

Creed, Barbara. 1993. *The Monstrous-Feminine: Film, Feminism, Psychoanalysis*. London: Routledge.

Creedon, Pamela J. 1993. *Women in Mass Communication*. 2d ed. Thousand Oaks, Calif.: Sage.

Crimp, Douglas, ed. 1988. *AIDS: Cultural Analysis/Cultural Activism*. Cambridge, Mass.: MIT Press.

Crook, Stephen, Jan Pakulski, and Malcolm Waters, eds. 1992. *Postmodernization: Change in Advanced Society*. London: Sage.

Cross, Gary. 1993. *Time and Money: The Making of a Consumer Culture*. London: Routledge.

Culler, Jonathan. 1975. *Structuralist Poetics: Structuralism, Linguistics and the Study of Literature*. Ithaca, N.Y.: Cornell University Press.

———. 1981. *The Pursuit of Signs*. Ithaca, N.Y.: Cornell University Press.

Danesi, Marcel. 1994. *Messages and Meanings: An Introduction to Semiotics*. Toronto: Canadian Scholars Press.

Danesi, Marcel, and Donato Santeramo, eds. 1992. *Introducing Semiotics: An Anthology of Readings*. Toronto: Canadian Scholars Press.

Davies, Christie. 2001. *The Mirth of Nations*. Piscataway, N.J.: Transaction.

Davis, Robert Con, and Ronald Schleifer. 1991. *Criticism and Culture*. London: Longman.

Dayan, Daniel, and Elihu Katz. 1987. "Television Ceremonial Events." In *Television in Society*, ed. Arthur Asa Berger. New Brunswick, N.J.: Transaction.

————. 1992. *Media Events: The Live Broadcasting of History*. Cambridge, Mass.: Harvard University Press.

DeFleur, Melvin L., and Otto N. Larsen. 1987. *The Flow of Information: An Experiment in Mass Communication*. New Brunswick, N.J.: Transaction.

Denney, Reuel. 1989. *The Astonished Muse*. New Brunswick, N.J.: Transaction.

Denzin, Norman K. 1991. *Images of Postmodern Society: Social Theory and Contemporary Cinema*. London: Sage.

Doane, Mary Ann. 1987. *The Desire to Desire: The Woman's Film of the 1940s*. Bloomington: Indiana University Press.

————. 1991. *Femmes Fatales*. New York: Routledge.

Donald, James, and Stuart Hall, eds. 1985. *Politics and Ideology*. Bristol, Pa.: Taylor & Francis.

Duncan, Hugh Dalziel. 1985. *Communication and the Social Order*. New Brunswick, N.J.: Transaction.

Dundes, Alan. 1987. *Cracking Jokes: Studies in Sick Humor Cycles and Stereotypes*. Berkeley, Calif.: Ten Speed Press.

Dworkin, Dennis L., and Leslie G. Roman. 1992. *Views beyond the Border Country: Raymond Williams and Cultural Politics*. New York: Routledge.

Dyer, Richard. 1993. *The Matter of Images: Essays on Representations*. London: Routledge.

Eagleton, Terry. 1983. *Literary Theory: An Introduction*. Minneapolis: University of Minnesota Press.

Easthope, Anthony. 1991. *Literary into Cultural Studies*. London: Routledge.

Eco, Umberto. 1984. *The Role of the Reader*. Bloomington: Indiana University Press.

Ehrmann, Jacques, ed. 1970. *Structuralism*. Garden City, N.Y.: Anchor.

Esslin, Martin. 2001. *The Age of Television*. Piscataway, N.J.: Transaction.

Ettema, James S., and D. Charles Whitney, eds. 1994. *Audiencemaking: How the Media Create the Audience*. Thousand Oaks, Calif.: Sage.

Ewen, Stuart. 1976. *Captains of Consciousness*. New York: McGraw-Hill.

Ewen, Stuart, and Elizabeth Ewen. 1982. *Channels of Desire: Mass Images and the Shaping of American Consciousness*. New York: McGraw-Hill.

Falk, Pasi, and Colin Campbell, eds. 1997. *The Shopping Experience*. London: Sage.

Featherstone, Mike. 1991. *Consumer Culture and Postmodernism*. London: Sage.

Fiske, John. 1989. *Understanding Popular Culture*. London: Routledge.

Fiske, John, and John Hartley. 1978. *Reading Television*. London: Methuen.

Fjellman, Stephen M. 1992. *Vinyl Leaves: Walt Disney World and America*. Boulder, Colo.: Westview.

Fox, Roy E. 2000. *Harvesting Minds: How TV Commercials Control Kids*. Westport, Conn.: Greenwood.

Franklin, Sarah, Celia Lury, and Jackie Stacey. 1992. *Off-Centre: Feminism and Cultural Studies*. London: Routledge.

Freud, Sigmund. 1965. *The Interpretation of Dreams*. Trans. James Strachey. New York: Avon.

Frith, Simon. 1981. *Sound Effects: Youth, Leisure and the Politics of Rock and Roll*. New York: Pantheon.

Frye, Northrop. 1957. *Anatomy of Criticism*. Princeton, N.J.: Princeton University Press.

Gandelman, Claude. 1991. *Reading Pictures, Viewing Texts*. Bloomington: Indiana University Press.

Garber, Marjorie, Jann Matlock, and Rebecca Walkowtiz, eds. 1993. *Media Spectacles*. New York: Routledge.

Garber, Marjorie, Pratibha Parmar, and John Greyson, eds. 1993. *Queer Looks: Perspectives on Lesbian and Gay Film and Video*. New York: Routledge.

Gitlin, Todd. 1985. *Inside Prime Time*. New York: Pantheon.

Gronbeck, Bruce, Thomas J. Farrell, and Paul A. Soukup, eds. 1991. *Media, Consciousness and Culture: Explorations of Walter Ong's Thought*. Newbury Park, Calif.: Sage.

Grossberg, Lawrence. 1992. *We Gotta Get Out of This Place: Popular Conservatism and Postmodern Culture*. New York: Routledge.

Grossberg, Lawrence, Cary Nelson, and Paula Treicher. 1991. *Cultural Studies*. New York: Routledge.

Gumbrecht, Hansl Ulrich. 1992. *Making Sense in Life and Literature*. Trans. Glen Burns. Minneapolis: University of Minnesota Press.

Gurke, Lisa Schauber. 1988. *The Meaning of Media Events: Broadcasting History*. Hamburg: Zaftig.

Habermas, Jürgen. 1989. *The New Conservatism: Cultural Criticism and the Historians' Debate*. Trans. Shierry Weber Nicholsen. Minneapolis: University of Minnesota Press.

Haddley-Lassiter, Nigel. 1992. *X-Effects*. London: Routledge.

———. 1996. *The Process of Communication: Who Says What to Whom in Which Channel with X Effects*. London: Bisto.

Hall, Stuart. 1988. *The Hard Road to Renewal*. London: Verso.

Hall, Stuart, and Paddy Whannel. 1967. *The Popular Arts: A Critical Guide to the Mass Media*. Boston: Beacon.

Hartley, John. 1992a. *The Politics of Pictures: The Creation of the Public in the Age of Popular Media*. London: Routledge.

———. 1992b. *Tele-ology: Studies in Television*. London: Routledge.

Haug, W. F. 1971. *Critique of Commodity Aesthetics: Appearance, Sexuality and Advertising in Capitalist Society*. Trans. Robert Bock. Minneapolis: University of Minnesota Press.

———. 1987. *Commodity Aesthetics, Ideology and Culture*. New York: International General.

Hoggart, Richard. 1992. *The Uses of Literacy*. New Brunswick, N.J.: Transaction.

Hoover, Stewart M. 1988. *Mass Media Religion: The Social Sources of the Electronic Church*. Newbury Park, Calif.: Sage.

Jacobs, Norman, ed. 1992. *Mass Media in Modern Society*. New Brunswick, N.J.: Transaction.

Jakobson, Roman. 1985. *Verbal Art, Verbal Sign, Verbal Time*. Ed. Krystyna Pomorska and Stephen Rudy. Minneapolis: University of Minnesota Press.

Jally, Sut, and Justin Lewis. 1992. *Enlightened Racism*: The Cosby Show, *Audiences and the Myth of the American Dream*. Boulder, Colo.: Westview.

Jameson, Frederic. 1992a. *The Geopolitical Aesthetic: Cinema and Space in the World System*. Bloomington: Indiana University Press.

———. 1992b. *Signatures of the Visible*. New York: Routledge.

Jauss, Hans Robert. 1982. *Toward an Aesthetic of Reception*. Trans. Timothy Bahti. Minneapolis: University of Minnesota Press.

Jensen, Joli. 1990. *Redeeming Modernity: Contradictions in Media Criticism*. Newbury Park, Calif.: Sage.

Jones, Steve. 1992. *Rock Formation: Music, Technology and Mass Communication*. Thousand Oaks, Calif.: Sage.

Jones, Steven G., ed. 1994. *Cybersociety: Computer-Mediated Communication and Community*. Thousand Oaks, Calif.: Sage.

Jowett, Garth, and James M. Linton. 1989. *Movies as Mass Communication*. Newbury Park, Calif.: Sage.

Jowett, Garth S., and Victoria O'Donnell. 1992. *Propaganda and Persuasion*. 2d ed. Thousand Oaks, Calif.: Sage.

Jung, Carl G., ed. 1968. *Man and His Symbols*. New York: Dell.

Kellner, Douglas. 1992. *The Persian Gulf TV War*. Boulder, Colo.: Westview.

———. 2001. *Grand Theft 2000: Media Spectacle and a Stolen Election*. Lanham, Md.: Rowman & Littlefield.

Korzenny, Felix, and Stella Ting-Toomey, eds. 1992. *Mass Media Effects across Cultures.* Newbury Park, Calif.: Sage.

Lang, Kurt, and Gladys Engel Lang. 2001. *Television and Politics.* New Brunswick, N.J.: Transaction.

Laurentis, Teresa de. 1984. *Alice Doesn't: Feminism, Semiotics, Cinema.* Bloomington: Indiana University Press.

————. 1987. *Technologies of Gender: Essays on Theory, Film and Fiction.* Bloomington: Indiana University Press.

Lazere, Donald, ed. 1987. *America Media and Mass Culture: Left Perspectives.* Berkeley: University of California Press.

LeFebvre, Henri. 1984. *Everyday Life in the Modern World.* Trans. Sacha Rabinovitch. New Brunswick, N.J.: Transaction.

Levy, Mark R., and Michael Gurevitch, eds. 1994. *Defining Media Studies: Reflections on the Future of the Field.* New York: Oxford University Press.

Lipsitz, George. 1989. *Time Passages: Collective Memory and American Popular Culture.* Minneapolis: University of Minnesota Press.

Lotman, Yuri M. 1976. *Semiotics of Cinema.* Ann Arbor: Michigan Slavic Contributions.

————. 1977. *The Structure of the Artistic Text.* Ann Arbor: Michigan Slavic Contributions.

Lull, James. 1991. *Popular Music and Communication.* Thousand Oaks, Calif.: Sage.

Lunenfeld, Peter, ed. 1999. *The Digital Dialectic: New Essays on New Media.* Cambridge, Mass.: MIT Press.

————. 2000. *Snap to Grid: A User's Guide to Digital Arts, Media, and Cultures.* Cambridge, Mass.: MIT Press

Lyotard, Jean-François. 1984. *The Postmodern Condition: A Report on Knowledge.* Minneapolis: University of Minnesota Press.

MacCannell, Dean, and Juliet Flower MacCannell. 1982. *The Time of the Sign: A Semiotic Interpretation of Modern Culture.* Bloomington: Indiana University Press.

MacDonald, J. Fred. 1994. *One Nation under Television.* Chicago: Nelson-Hall.

Mandel, Ernest. 1985. *Delightful Murder: A Social History of the Crime Story.* Minneapolis: University of Minnesota Press.

Martin-Barbero, Jesus. 1993. *Communication, Culture, and Hegemony: From the Media to Mediations.* Thousand Oaks, Calif.: Sage.

Mattelart, Armand, and Michele Mattelart. 1992. *Rethinking Media Theory.* Trans. James A. Cohen and Marina Urquidi. Minneapolis: University of Minnesota Press.

————. 1998. *Theories of Communication: A Short Introduction.* Thousand Oaks, Calif.: Sage.

McCue, Greg, with Clive Bloom. 1993. *Dark Knights: The New Comics in Context.* Boulder, Colo.: Westview.

McLuhan, Marshall. 1965. *Understanding Media: The Extensions of Man.* New York: McGraw-Hill.

———. 1970. *Culture Is Our Business.* New York: McGraw-Hill.

McLuhan, Marshall, and Quentin Fiore. 1967. *The Medium Is the Massage.* New York: Bantam.

McQuail, Denis. 1992. *Media Performance: Mass Communication and the Public Interest.* Thousand Oaks, Calif.: Sage.

———. 2000. *McQuail's Mass Communication Theory: An Introduction.* 4th ed. Thousand Oaks, Calif.: Sage.

Mellencamp, Patricia. 1990a. *Indiscretions: Avant-Garde Film, Video and Feminism.* Bloomington: Indiana University Press.

———, ed. 1990b. *Logics of Television: Essays in Cultural Criticism.* Bloomington: Indiana University Press.

Messaris, Paul. 1994. *Visual Literacy: Image, Mind and Reality.* Boulder, Colo.: Westview.

———. 1997. *Visual Persuasion.* Thousand Oaks, Calif.: Sage.

Mindess, Harvey. 1971. *Laughter and Liberation.* Los Angeles: Nash.

Modleski, Tania. 1984. *Loving with a Vengeance: Mass-Produced Fantasies for Women.* New York: Routledge.

———, ed. 1986. *Studies in Entertainment: Critical Approaches to Mass Culture.* Bloomington: Indiana University Press.

———. 1988. *The Women Who Knew Too Much: Hitchcock and Feminist Theory.* New York: Routledge.

Moores, Shaun. 1994. *Interpreting Audiences: The Ethnography of Media Consumption.* Thousand Oaks, Calif.: Sage.

Morley, David. 1988. *Family Television: Cultural Power and Domestic Leisure.* London: Routledge.

———. 1993. *Television Audiences and Cultural Studies.* London: Routledge.

Mulvey, Laura. 1989. *Visual and Other Pleasures.* Bloomington: Indiana University Press.

Nagoya, Hideo. 1998. *In a Garden.* Tokyo: Nishin.

Naremore, James, and Patrick Brantlinger, eds. 1991. *Modernity and Mass Culture.* Bloomington: Indiana University Press.

Nash, Christopher, ed. 1990. *Narrative in Culture.* London: Routledge.

Nehring, Neil. 1997. *Popular Music, Gender, and Postmodernism.* Thousand Oaks, Calif.: Sage.

Nichols, Bill. 1981. *Ideology and the Image: Social Representation in the Cinema and Other Media.* Bloomington: Indiana University Press.

————. 1992. *Representing Reality: Issues and Concepts in Documentary*. Bloomington: Indiana University Press.

Penley, Constance. 1989. *The Future of an Illusion: Film, Feminism and Psychoanalysis*. Minneapolis: University of Minnesota Press.

Powell, Chris, and George E. C. Paton, eds. 1988. *Humour in Society: Resistance and Control*. New York: St. Martin's.

Prindle, David. F. 1993. *Risky Business: The Political Economy of Hollywood*. Boulder, Colo.: Westview.

Propp, Vladimir. 1973. *Morphology of the Folk Tale*. 2d ed. Austin: University of Texas Press.

————. 1984. *Theory and History of Folklore*. Trans. Ariadna Y. Martin and Richard P. Martin. Minneapolis: University of Minnesota Press.

Ramet, Sabrina Petra, ed. 1993. *Rocking the State: Rock Music and Politics in Eastern Europe and the Soviet Union*. Boulder, Colo.: Westview.

Real, Michael R. 1989. *Supermedia: A Cultural Studies Approach*. Newbury Park, Calif.: Sage.

Reinelt, Janelle G., and Joseph R. Roach, eds. 1993. *Critical Theory and Performance*. Ann Arbor: University of Michigan Press.

Richter, Mischa, and Harald Bakken. 1992. *The Cartoonist's Muse: A Guide to Generating and Developing Creative Ideas*. Chicago: Contemporary.

Ryan, Michael, and Douglas Kellner. 1988. *Camera Politica: The Politics and Ideology and Contemporary Hollywood Film*. Bloomington: Indiana University Press.

Sabin, Roger. 1993. *Adult Comics: An Introduction*. London: Routledge.

Said, Edward. 1983. *The World, the Text, and the Critic*. Cambridge, Mass.: Harvard University Press.

Saint-Martin, Fernande. 1990. *Semiotics of Visual Language*. Bloomington: Indiana University Press.

Saussure, Ferdinand de. 1966. *Course in General Linguistics*. Trans. Wade Baskin. New York: McGraw-Hill.

Schechner, Richard. 1993. *The Future of Ritual: Writings on Culture and Performance*. London: Routledge.

Schostak, John. 1993. *Dirty Marks: The Education of Self, Media and Popular Culture*. Boulder, Colo.: Westview.

Schwichtenberg, Cathy, ed. *The Madonna Collection*. Boulder, Colo.: Westview.

Seldes, Gilbert. 1994. *The Public Arts*. New Brunswick, N.J.: Transaction.

Simmul, Jean-Georg. 1981. *The System of Things*. Paris: University of Paris Press.

————. 1988. *The Evangelical Hamburger*. London: Boeuf-hache.

————. 1989. *A Critique of the Significance of the Sign*. Paris: Clochard.

————. 1995. *New Perspectives on the Consumer Society.* Paris: Hermes.

Skovman, Michael, ed. N.d. *Media Fictions.* Aarhus, Denmark: Aarhus University Press.

Smith, Gary, ed. 1991. *On Walter Benjamin: Critical Essays and Recollections.* Cambridge, Mass.: MIT Press.

Smith, Paul. 1988. *Discerning the Subject.* Minneapolis: University of Minnesota Press.

Steidman, Steven. 1993. *Romantic Longings: Love in America 1830–1980.* New York: Routledge.

Stephenson, William. 1988. *The Play Theory of Mass Communication.* New Brunswick, N.J.: Transaction.

Szondi, Peter. 1986. *On Textual Understanding.* Trans. Harvey Mendelsohn. Minneapolis: University of Minnesota Press.

Thaler, Paul. 1997. *The Spectacle: Media and the Making of the O.J. Simpson Story.* Westport, Conn.: Greenwood.

Todorov, Tzvetan. 1975. *The Fantastic: A Structural Approach to a Literary Genre.* Trans. Richard Howard. Ithaca, N.Y.: Cornell University Press.

————. 1981. *Introduction to Poetics.* Trans. Richard Howard. Minneapolis: University of Minnesota Press.

————. 1984. *Mikhail Bakhtin: The Dialogical Principle.* Minneapolis: University of Minnesota Press.

Traube, Elizabeth G. 1982. *Dreaming Identities: Class, Gender, and Generation in the 1980s Hollywood Movies.* Boulder, Colo.: Westview.

Turner, Bryan S. 1990. *Theories of Modernity and Postmodernity.* London: Sage.

Van Zoonen, Liesbet. 1994. *Feminist Media Studies.* Thousand Oaks, Calif.: Sage.

Vološinova, Mikhaila Blotnik-Kiev. 1992. *Conversationalism: The Importance of Dialogue in Communication.* Tartu: Pelmenyii.

Weibel, Kathryn. 1977. *Mirror Mirror: Images of Women Reflected in Popular Culture.* Garden City, N.Y.: Anchor.

Weimann, Gabriel. 1999. *Communicating Unreality: Modern Media and the Reconstruction of Reality.* Thousand Oaks, Calif.: Sage.

Wernick, Andrew. 1991. *Promotional Culture.* London: Sage.

Wicks, Robert H. 2001. *Understanding Audiences.* Mahwah, N.J.: Erlbaum.

Willemen, Paul. 1993. *Looks and Frictions: Essays in Cultural Studies and Film Theory.* Bloomington: Indiana University Press.

Williams, Raymond. 1958. *Culture and Society: 1780–1950.* New York: Columbia University Press.

————. 1976. *Keywords.* New York: Oxford University Press.

————. 1977. *Marxism and Literature.* New York: Oxford University Press.

Williams, Rosalind. 1990. *Notes on the Underground: An Essay on Technology, Society and the Imagination.* Cambridge, Mass.: MIT Press.

Williamson, Judith. 1978. *Decoding Advertisements: Ideology and Meaning in Advertising.* London: Boyars.

Willis, Paul. 1990. *Common Culture: Symbolic Work at Play in the Everyday Cultures of the Young.* Boulder, Colo.: Westview.

Wilson, Clint C., and Felix Gutierrez. 1985. *Minorities and Media: Diversity and the End of Mass Communication.* Thousand Oaks, Calif.: Sage.

Winick, Charles. 1994. *Desexualization in American Life: The New People.* New Brunswick, N.J.: Transaction.

Wollen, Peter. 1972. *Signs and Meaning in the Cinema.* Bloomington: Indiana University Press.

————. 1993. *Raiding the Icebox: Reflections on Twentieth-Century Culture.* Bloomington: Indiana University Press.

Wright, Will. 1975. *Sixguns and Society: A Structural Study of the Western.* Berkeley: University of California Press.

Zizek, Slavoi. 1991. *Looking Awry: An Introduction to Jacques Lacan through Popular Culture.* Cambridge, Mass.: MIT Press.

Index

advertising: influence of, 54; McLuhan's use of, 10
America: advertising and consumer culture, 16; culture of consumption, 111; dining versus eating, 18; high-status and low-status foods, 19; humor and criminality, 21–22; infantile starvation and freezers, 16; motels in, 14–15; muscle cars, 15; sexual identity of appliances, 15; shopping malls in, 88; status of foods, 17–21; white balloon bread and ideology, 17
American Sociological Review, 76
Audiences: characteristics of, 93; not simple consumers, 93; source, channel, and message variables, 93
Auster, Paul, 65

Bakhtin, Mikhail, 86
Ball-Rokeach, Sandra, 24, 93
Bass, A. Z., 90
Benson, Thomas W., 94
Berelson, Bernard, 11
Blondie, 10
Booth, Wayne, 94
Boylan, James, 93

Cantor, Muriel, 93
collective representations, 101–102
comedy, 108
communication process, 48
communication theory: agenda setting, 32; hypodermic theory, 31; interpersonal, 109. *See* mass communication
cultural studies, 10
Current Issues in Higher Education (Gerbner), 42

Davison, W. Phillips, 93
DeFleur, Melvin L., 24, 86
dialogic theory: creativity and, 44; nature of conversation, 44–45
Dinh, Tran Van, "On Critical and Administrative Research: A New Critical Analysis," 104

Eyal, Chaim, 90

Fiske, John, xvi
Freud, Sigmund, 47
Freudian theory: id, ego, and superego, 47; ideological motif in, 47; Oedipus complex, 47; power of sexual instinct, 47

141

About the Author

Arthur Asa Berger was born in Boston in 1933. He graduated from the University of Massachusetts, where he majored in literature, in 1954. He went on for an M.A. degree in journalism and creative writing from the University of Iowa in 1956. He was drafted shortly after graduating from Iowa and served in the U.S. Army in the Military District of Washington in Washington, D.C., where he was a feature writer and speech writer in the District's Public Information Office. He also wrote on high school sports for *The Washington Post* on weekend evenings.

Berger spent a year touring Europe after he got out of the army, worked in New York for a year, and then went to the University of Minnesota, where he received a Ph.D. in American studies in 1965. He wrote his dissertation on the comic strip *Li'l Abner*. He took a year out of his studies to teach in Italy. In 1963–64, he had a Fulbright to Italy and taught at the University of Milan.

After graduating from Minnesota, he went to San Francisco State University, where he remained, except for a year spent as visiting professor at the Annenberg School for Communication at the University of Southern California in Los Angeles. Berger took semiretirement from San Francisco State University in 1998.

He is the author of more than one hundred articles, countless book reviews, and more than forty books on the mass media, popular culture, humor, and everyday life. Among his books are *Media Analysis Techniques*, *Media Research Techniques*, *Bloom's Morning*, *The Genius of the Jewish Joke*, *Cultural Criticism*, *Jewish Jesters*, *The Art of Comedy Writing*, and *Ads, Fads, and Consumer Culture*. His books have been translated into German, Swedish, Italian, Korean, Chinese, and Indonesian. He has lectured in many countries, such as England, France, Italy, Germany, Finland, Denmark, Sweden, Norway, Brazil, Thailand, China, and Korea.

In recent years, Berger has written a number of humorous academic mysteries that also can function as textbooks. He has written a mystery on postmodernism, *Postmortem for a Postmodernist*; a mystery on different ways of interpreting *Hamlet*, *The Hamlet Case*; and two mysteries about humor, *Die Laughing* and *The Aristotle Case*.

Berger is married, has two children and one grandchild, and lives in Mill Valley, California. His E-mail address is aberger@sfsu.edu.